WYLDE RIDE:

A HORSEMAN'S STORY

WYLDE RIDE:
A HORSEMAN'S STORY

By
JOE DOTOLI

With a foreword by
MEREDITH MICHAELS-BEERBAUM

Order this book online at www.trafford.com
or email orders@trafford.com

Most Trafford titles are also available at major online book retailers.

Printed in the United States of America.

ISBN: 978-1-4269-3604-3 (soft)
ISBN: 978-1-4269-3605-0 (hard)

Library of Congress Control Number: 2010909428

*Our mission is to efficiently provide the world's finest, most comprehensive book publishing
service, enabling every author to experience success. To find out how to publish your book,
your way, and have it available worldwide, visit us online at www.trafford.com*

Trafford rev. 8/4/2010

Trafford
PUBLISHING®   www.trafford.com

North America & international
toll-free: 1 888 232 4444 (USA & Canada)
phone: 250 383 6864 ♦ fax: 812 355 4082

For my girls;
Fran, Annie, Julia and Nora

Never let the fear of striking out get in your way.

George Herman "Babe" Ruth

Contents

Foreword

When Joe Dotoli asked me to write the foreword for his upcoming book about Peter Wylde, I felt not only honored but excited to read the story, told from its true beginning, of my longtime friend. Throughout our careers, Peter and I have shared many similar experiences. We are both American riders who left the comfort and security of the American horse world to jump head first into the demanding, exciting and highly competitive sport of international Show Jumping. At that time, this was completely unheard of, as there were no Americans competing at the top level in Europe.

Though Americans, Peter and I actually first met each other in Europe. We quickly became friends, identifying and sympathizing with each other's struggles and victories. We learned how difficult survival in the sport would be for us, and how brutally unforgiving the worst moments could be. But we loved the excitement and dimension of European competition, and the wonderful, dynamic atmosphere. Looking back, it is easy to say that our paths were well chosen. We have both enjoyed our fair share of successes, and we have both had the honor of representing our countries as medalists in the world's most prestigious Show Jumping Championship events. But I know how difficult that life-changing decision was, to move from the known into the complete unknown. Perhaps more than anyone, I know how many sacrifices Peter made to become the athlete that he is today.

My first memories of Peter Wylde were from reading about him winning the Maclay Finals at Madison Square Garden. I will never forget how, as an aspiring young rider, I flipped through the pages of *The Chronicle of the Horse* magazine and looked in awe at this young man who sat so beautifully on his striking white horse. I remember reading about how flawlessly he executed the courses with invisible aids and made riding seem so easy and rhythmical. I remember thinking that is exactly what I wanted to be-- just like Peter Wylde-- the winner of the Maclay finals--so elegant, so effortless.

Needless to say, I never did win the Maclay finals, nor did I, as an equitation rider, ever come close to resembling Peter's classic riding style and beauty on a horse. But years later, having experienced many victories and defeats of my own, and having traveled far, far away from my California roots, I had the pleasure of meeting Peter Wylde in Europe. Our friendship grew quickly as we realized how very alike our life experiences had been. As young riders, Peter and I had learned similar systems. Peter began riding under the tutelage of Fran and Joe Dotoli. I had started my riding at Foxfield, and continued my training with Karen Healey and George Morris. With great teachers, we had both been taught riding and horsemanship and the proper way to do things-- how to provide for horses with the best vets, shoers and stable management imaginable. We knew how important it was to be precise and meticulous in our care, feeding and training. We had learned discipline. We had been in stables where horses' manes laid perfectly flat with not a hair out of place. We had seen brass polished on tack trunks until it glistened and you could see your reflection in it. There was not a speck of dust on the stable floors where we were taught. That was why I still chuckle today when I think what it was like for Peter when he arrived in Europe and went to work for a "real" horse dealer.

There was nothing glamorous about a dealing stable. There was no polished brass. There were no manicured lawns. It was only about riding horses, showing horses, and selling horses. I think Peter, who was so exact in his care for horses, felt like someone had thrown a barrel full of ice water over his head. He saw horses ridden till hot and sweaty and then put away wet with no bandages. He told me stories about two horses bedded in one stall for days on end, simply because there were no more stalls. He told me about horses left on the walking machine overnight because the stalls were full and there was no more room. But his shock and horror finally reached its pinnacle when he called and told me that the management had cutback on costs and therefore there would be no more shavings or straw purchased. Peter was horrified to hear that he was supposed to use dirt from the indoor ring to bed his horses!

Peter had been presented with a new outlook on the sport and stable management. Horses were cared for at the dealer's stable, but without the luxuries Peter had come to know. Peter realized that most of the riders there were not concerned with the details of stable management. They wanted their horses to perform in the ring and they wanted to win. Otherwise, the other employed riders were given the better horses. Peter was just one of many and he learned that it was time to fend for himself. It was sink or swim. There were high expectations, and very little sympathy for failure. I can only imagine how different this was from the warm, comfortable, family atmosphere that Fran and Joe had provided. But this experience made him a better rider and a more intense competitor. It also made him more determined than ever to return to the standard of horse care with which he grew up and had learned to cherish.

Peter moved on from the dealing stable and began the trek of building his own stable. When doing so, he never forgot his background, his upbringing. He never forgot the welfare of the horse. He was forced to make new choices. He had stepped out of his protective cocoon and was seeing the horse world with new eyes. He had to sift through the bad and take out the good. He did this and built himself a successful stable-- riding, training and competing at the very top level.

I'll never forget when Peter competed at the World Championships in Jerez with Fein Cera. The Germans had decided not to include me on their team at the WEG that year with the then nine-year-old Shutterfly. Instead, my wonderful husband Markus took me on vacation to Sardenia, Italy, to distract and console me. In between my soothing swims in the Mediterranean, I would listen for my phone and anxiously await phone calls from Peter updating me with the latest from Jerez. I couldn't believe it when he made it to the final four! I still remember how nervous Peter was during the horse change and how he told me that Eric Navet's horse presented the biggest challenge. After attempting one of the warm-up jumps on Navet's horse and having it down because the horse pulled him underneath the fence, Peter turned to his mentor Conrad Homfeld for well-needed advice. Conrad was silent and thought for a moment before he calmly addressed Peter's nervous and frightful expression, "How about... find a better distance?" I love the wise simplicity spoken so precisely by one of the world's best. A small jolt of reality helped Peter refocus and take home the bronze medal.

To this day, Peter and I love meeting each other at the shows and discussing all the intricacies of our sport. We love watching the best in the world and dissecting their rounds in effort to discover their secrets to success. We discuss the future of our sport, the positive and the negative. We try to help each other with each other's horses and riding, offering comments or tips. And through it all, Peter's thirst for knowledge has never wavered. He has asked questions and has implemented solutions. He has joined committees and spoken out for the betterment of the sport. He has not only established himself as a horseman and a rider, but as a valuable player in the sport who has something worthy to contribute.

I am not sure which part of Peter Wylde I can say I admire most. The rider who has won medals at Championship events? Or the rider who can develop a young horse to the top level of show jumping? Perhaps it is the horseman who can run a top class stable with the best horse care possible and train young riders? Maybe it is the relentless athlete who can sit in endless meetings determined to improve our sport? I think it is a combination of all these things, of the boy who won the Maclay Finals at age sixteen and went on to dedicate his life to the love of the horse. Peter is an inspiration. Peter followed his dreams and pursued the quest for knowledge through all its hills and valleys to become one of the best in our sport.

Acknowledgements

I basically wrote every word of this book sitting at my computer. There wasn't much need for research, since this manuscript was born of a jumble of stories rattling around in my head for most of my life. The only actual research I did was some fact-finding and uncovering the whereabouts of photographers whom I had not seen or heard of in many years to see if it would be all right to use their pictures in the book. I must admit to being shocked at how possible the Internet made that job. The photographers were all incredibly helpful, and I thank them all. It was fun reconnecting with people like Judith Buck, whom I have not spoken to for more than twenty years, but who could not have been more gracious. I can still so clearly remember her flipping one of her shoes in the air when she wanted to get a horse to put his ears up, all the while looking through the camera lens.

I also want to thank Steven Price, who took time from his busy schedule to edit a friend's book. I appreciate him not being deterred by his over qualification. Thank you to my sister-in-law, Mary Cunning for patiently answering all the "How do I make this computer do…" questions, and to Jess Martin (another one of our terrific former students) for putting it all into a form that the publisher could actually work with. Of course, how can I thank Meredith Michaels-Beerbaum enough for writing such a warm, funny and insightful foreword.

More to the point of who to thank for the completion of my book, are those who put the many stories in my head in the first place. Nothing would have been possible without all the wonderful horses that have been part of our lives. There are those that had long careers and well deserved retirements, like Native Surf (Surf), Devil's River (Devil), Catch of the Day

(Tuna), Sundance (Butch), Niatross (Sam) and Rhodes (Rhodes). There were the ones that did so very much for us but, in the end, we lost contact with after they were sold; horses like the great Baryshnikov (Mischa). I hope they continued to get the respect they deserved. Finally, there are the ones whose careers and even their lives were cut short trying to do what we asked of them, like old Rusty and the magnificent Legendary (Sting). I miss them all. They are what make this sport possible and special.

Then, there are the riders who found their way to our stable. Many have followed us into the horse business. Peter and our own daughter Annie of course, but there are many others; Claire (Desautels) Heisler, Leslie Kogos, Wendy Barquin, Lili (Bieler) Biedermann, Vanessa Waltz, Mindy Hinsdale, Bill Cooney, Laena Romond, Molly Kenney, Amanda Steege, Kristy Downing, and Ashley (Henderson) Stewart, among others. Many more continue to ride as amateurs, like Beth (McCombs) Westvold, Jeannine Cash and Julie (Taylor) Calder. Many keep in contact with us and tell us that their children carry on the tradition. Additionally, there are those who started out as working students or to whom we gave their first job, that have gone on to do great things; people like James Lala, Cathy Fletcher, and Lori Cramer. They all have been important to these stories and to our lives.

Finally I need to thank my teachers; Maryanne English, who piqued my interest in horses, Harold Belliveau who allowed me to make The Broken Wheel Ranch my second home and first taught me the importance of being a horseman, and Major Mike Antoniewicz, next to my father the most influential man in my life. Of course the person who taught me the most about horses is my partner of forty-one years, Fran. She came from a different horse background than I did. She was trained by some of the greats of the sport including; Anna Powers Rowe, Elaine (Moore) Moffat, and the legend of legends, Gordon Wright. She never hesitated to share her knowledge with me or our students. She is the best teacher I have ever known, simply the best.

*   *   *   *

Recently, I was watching The Today Show on morning television (I often leave it on while we organize our day). Marlo Thomas was promoting the wonderful work she does raising money for research at Saint Jude Children's Hospital, much the same way her comedian father Danny did when he was alive. She had two children from the hospital with her, one of them was a girl around thirteen or fourteen who was fighting her battle with cancer. At the end of the interview with Ms. Thomas, Matt Lauer turned to the girl and asked what she would like to do in the future. The girl answered that she loved horses and hoped some day to ride in the Olympics. It stopped me. Her answer was so sincere and honest. As I looked at that beautiful young girl on the television I thought "wouldn't it be great if she got her chance some day". A quotation from Winston Churchill tells us, "The outside of a horse is good for the inside of a man". The thought of riding again one day was certainly helping this brave child.

Preface

I am a horseman! That is not my occupation; it is my life. For more than forty years my wife Fran and I have centered our lives around these magnificent animals. We have trained them and the people who ride them. We have stayed home on Christmas and Thanksgiving, and all of the other holidays, because someone had to be there. We have been inspired by the efforts of the great ones, and disappointed by the failures of the average ones. We have tended to them all night when they were sick, and buried them when they died. Horses are not like ice skates that can be hung up on a hook when you want to do something else. Horses must be cared for everyday, even when it is inconvenient. Being a horseman cannot be measured in hours, days, months, or years; it is a vocation. Without being ready to make that kind of sacrifice, that kind of commitment, you are not really a horseman. You may like horses, you may even own a horse, but you will never be a horseman.

There are horsemen and there are riders, and occasionally there is someone great enough to excel at both. This is a story of one such person, and our longtime relationship with him as his trainers and friends. If you are a basketball fan, you can read books about the life of Michael Jordan, Larry Bird, or Magic Johnson. You can read what they were like growing up, their work ethic, what roadblocks they overcame. You can learn what it finally meant to them to succeed. You can be inspired. There are similar stories in almost every sport, but horse books seem to focus on "how to": how to ride, how to jump, how to take care of your sick or injured horse, or how to manage your stable. I have never seen a book on the life of Bill

Steinkraus, George Morris, Conrad Homfeld, or any of the other giants of our sport.

Our horses don't fare much better. There is the occasional book or movie about race horses like Seabiscut, Pharlap and National Velvet, but the closest that show horses have come to stardom is the 1960 movie "The Horse with the Flying Tail", the story of Hugh Wiley's unlikely international show jumper, Nautical.

"How to" books are fine, they serve a noble purpose; to educate. However, they can't give inspiration. They can show you how to do it right, but they can't make you want to do it right, which is my reason for writing this book. Peter Wylde is a great rider, but more important to me he is an even greater horseman. His successes have never come at the expense of his horses. He views his accomplishments as those of his horses first and secondly his own. I hope that reading about his evolution into an equestrian superstar will make young riders want to do it right, that it will make them want to be horsemen first.

Sharing the Gift of Horsemanship

Thanksgiving day, 2005 was cold and grey. A bone-chilling wind pushed us along as we made the trek from our rental car to Peter's apartment, a magnificent three-story building in Maastricht, The Netherlands. What an unusual place to celebrate such a uniquely American holiday I thought. Our younger daughter, Julia, who was attending graduate school in Glasgow, working toward her masters degree in Fine Arts, had flown over from Scotland to join us. Fran and I were picked up at the airport by our older daughter, Annie. An accomplished horseman in her own right, Annie was working and living in Belgium. I was looking forward to us all being together for the first time in some months.

When we got to Peter's building, all four of us snuggled into the doorway to get out of the wind. Annie pushed the doorbell. "We don't want any, go away" kiddingly came a voice we all recognized as Peter's. The next instant, the buzzer sounded to let us in. We walked up one flight and found Peter and his mom, Seddon, who had arrived the day before from her home in Cambridge Massachusetts, at the top of the stairs, arms wide open. There were hugs and "happy Thanksgivings" all around, and then we went inside. Two other friends of Peter's had also been invited; David from Long Island, and Eduard, from Holland. As the others visited over a glass of wine in the kitchen, I looked around in the living room.

On a wall over the sofa was a frame that held a triangular shaped ribbon. Attached to the bottom point of the ribbon was a silver medal. The inscription on the brass plaque below read:

Individual and Team Silver Medalist
Pan American Games
Winnipeg, Alberta, Canada – 1999
Peter I. Wylde

A mahogany table in one corner of the room supported a beautiful bronze statue of two horses playing. The plate on its front read:

World Equestrian Games
Jerez, Spain
Best Horse in the Final
Fein Cera

Peter's individual Bronze Medal lay next to the statue in its own case. Another table at the far end of the room held a sculpture of a stylized horse head that was finished in gold leaf. It was the "Style of Riding" award from the Aachen Horse Show in Germany. With very little debate, Aachen is the greatest horse show in the world. Peter is the only American to have won this award. On display on one of the end tables next to the sofa was a replica of the 1982 Maclay trophy, symbolic of the United States Junior National Equitation Championship.

On the remaining wall was a picture of Peter's niece, Fiona. She was shown in profile, with an amazingly intense look for a child. She was proudly waving the American flag with both hands. Superimposed on the bottom of the print was:

Athens 2004

To the right of that picture was another of equal size and with the same framing, a close-up of Peter and Fein Cera. A smiling Peter is flashing the thumbs-up sign as he galloped across the Olympic stadium. Fein Cera, with only her head and neck showing, looked fantastic. Between the two images was centered another triangular ribbon, a blue one. On the bottom point, however, was attached a gold medal. It was the team gold medal from the 2004 Olympics in Athens, Greece.

It gave me chills to think that all his hard work had paid off and that he had established himself as one of the great American riders. He did it with a lot of hard work and determination, and he did it as a great horseman as well as a rider. It has been quite a journey.

It felt wonderful for us all to be together for Thanksgiving. When we sat down to the luxurious table that Peter had set, we raised our glasses and they gently clinked as we wished each other happy Thanksgiving. I thought how lucky I was, just a kid from the neighborhood who was fortunate enough to find a passion for horses, and find a life-long love with the same passion. Good fortune found Fran and me in a big way in the late seventies, when an incredibly talented twelve-year-old boy and his parents showed up at our stable and asked if we would train him. That little boy, of course, was Peter, and he took us to places that when I was a boy, I had never heard of. It was the beginning of a thirty-year relationship, the first half as his trainers, the second half as his friends and mentors. Yes, I suppose mentor is an appropriate term. I like the sound of that – mentor.

*   *   *   *

I grew up in Milton Massachusetts, a suburb of Boston. Even as a boy, I loved animals. We had a family dog whose name was Duke, and like most young boys and their dogs, Duke and I were inseparable. Along the way I kept a variety of other assorted creatures. I had an ant farm, and the occasional injured bird which of course died in captivity. My father once brought a baby alligator home from Florida as a gift (thankfully this practice is no longer legal) and I cared for it with such diligence that it grew to a length of four feet. It took both my brother and I to clean the old tub where it lived. I finally had to donate it to the Boston Museum of Science before it ate someone. At one point, I was stowing away a family of pet mice in the lower section of my parents' china cabinet. I lined the area with glass, cleaned it every day, and was quite proud of the fact that nobody had discovered the little hideaway. One day my mother smelled an odd odor and went investigating, that was not a good day. Horses, however, were foreign to me. Other than the primitive 1950's westerns that I saw on our black and white TV, the only experience I had with horses were a few times that my brother and I convinced my father to take us to the Blue Hills, a Massachusetts state preserve, for pony rides after going to the Rodeo which came to the old Boston Garden once a year in those days.

Maryanne English, was, and is, my sister Honey's best friend (Honey's name is actually Margaret, but nobody calls her that). Maryanne is a couple years older than Honey, who is three years my elder. Maryanne's father had been very successful as owner of a string of Irish pubs in Boston's ethnic neighborhoods. They lived at the top of the hill, on Pillon Road. Maryanne was the only person that I knew growing up, that had ever gone to Europe (the people I knew CAME FROM Europe, you didn't GO TO Europe). This was something that impressed me very much as a teen; that and the fact that she was very beautiful. Maryanne had attended graduate school in Germany to study for her master's degree in art history. While there, she was exposed to riding, and was "bitten by the bug". When she returned to the States, she bought a horse and kept it at a public boarding stable in the Blue Hills. She was also the only person I ever knew that owned a horse. One Saturday morning, when she was at our house, Maryanne asked me if I would like to go riding with her. I was about fifteen or sixteen years old at the time.

That first day of riding is one of my most vivid memories. Maryanne led the way on her horse; I followed on one that she rented for me. Everything about the experience, from the smell of the barn, to the feeling I got just being on a horse, told me that I found the place where I wanted to be. Our Saturday rides became fairly frequent. We would go out for an hour or two and usually stop for a cold drink or an ice cream and then Maryanne would drive me home. I loved everything about those days. She never had to ask twice.

It wasn't long before I began going to the barn, the Belliveau Riding Academy, on my own. I would hang around on weekends, helping out and hoping to get some free rides in exchange for leading a group of renters through the preserve. The most exciting time was Monday night when the stable's charismatic owner, Bushy Belliveau, hosted an auction. The most eclectic array of tack, equipment and horse care products ever assembled, followed by a few dozen horses, passed in front of Bushy in his role as auctioneer. The horses ranged from two-year-olds just off the track to hack horses from other rental barns to a few poor old or broken individuals headed for the "killers". I tried not to think about the latter, but it's a fact of life with horse auctions.

The auction barn was set up with a grandstand along one wall. On the other side was all the tack and other items to be auctioned off. Down the center, was a dirt corridor. The horses were paraded up and down this aisle-way while bidders shouted and argued with each other. The crowd was mostly men, usually dressed in some form of Western wear. I had my own cowboy boots, hat and chaps by then, and I fit right in, or at least I was convinced that I did.

Bushy stood in the middle of the auction barn and attested to all the wonderful qualities of each horse as he tried to raise the price. "He rides and drives; any child can ride him; he won fives races as a two-year-old". Bushy really didn't know much about any of the horses, but would say whatever he thought might make a sale. His biggest crowd-pleaser was to say, "If this hoss aint one hundred pacent sound, may the Lord strike me right here where I stand". Then Bushy would meekly roll his eyes toward the heavens, and take one step back. It brought the house down every time.

The most important thing to come out of my time at Belliveau Riding Academy, from my perspective, was meeting Bushy's younger brother, Harold. Bushy apparently had been quite a rider at one time, and he certainly had the outgoing personality. He would entertain all night long at the auctions and kept everyone smiling and laughing, but Harold was a horseman. Harold was very quiet, at first I almost had to pry information out of him, but he was the first person who I realized knew how a horse thinks. He was my first great influence as a horseman.

Harold owned a small hack and rental barn in Sharon, Massachusetts called the Broken Wheel Ranch. After spending some time with Harold at the auctions, I began to help him at the ranch on weekends. I mucked stalls, took groups out on the trails, and helped feed and water. I went every chance I got, often hitchhiking from Milton if I couldn't get a ride. Harold couldn't afford to pay me, but he gave me the occasional lesson, and I just loved being there

My favorite time at the barn was, and still is, evening feeding. At the ranch, like at most stables, it was ritualistic. The horses all got the same feed; the ponies were given lesser amounts. One can of Harold's special mix of oats, sweet-feed, and bran – in the winter months we added corn. They were the same large three quart cans that I used to see on the back shelves of my father's restaurant. When I went to the grain room to fill them, all the horses would begin to nicker and twirl around in their stalls. Water was first though, and the horses knew the routine. The upstairs of the barn had a water trough (actually it was an old bath tub) at the far end of the aisle. We began closest to the tub, Harold on one side and me on the other. The doors were opened one at a time, and the resident of the stall would walk smartly to the tub for a good long drink. Harold spoke to them in his quiet, gentle manner; "Come on Casey, get on back to your stall, you're just playing with the water now". Each horse would take its turn. Rusty was last, he lived in the stall closest to the door. Rusty had been with Harold a long time, he was Harold's favorite. "Come on old man, get yourself a drink". Rusty was the only one that got to stop and visit with the others on his way back to his stall, like a parent checking on the kids before bed.

Today, I would never think of having all the horses drink out of the same trough or of having them spend all night in their stalls without at least two clean buckets of water, but that was the way Harold did things, and everything seemed to work just fine.

Hay was next, and I would vault up the ladder to the hayloft and throw down enough bales to feed all the upstairs horses. Harold would pop the strings and start haying. The horses all stared out through their stall doors with anticipation. After that phase was complete, we headed to the grain room to get the cans of Harold's special mix. By pinching them together, I could carry two in each hand and so could Harold. Eight cans were just enough to feed upstairs. The process was repeated downstairs in the low ceiling, dark underbelly of the barn. Finally, we both grabbed a broom and swept.

Those moments after feeding time have always remained special for me. The horses have been cared for, they are calm and happy. The peaceful sound of horses rhythmically munching on their hay has become one of the joyous constants of my life. No matter what part of the world I would be in, or how luxurious the stables that I would one day work in, that moment, and those sounds remained my favorite time of the day and would always remind me why I do what I do.

As time went on, Harold let me show some of the horses. It took a lot of convincing, well, nagging really, but eventually we began heading to local horse shows with a little sorrel Quarter Horses named Pee Wee. I competed in Western shows, in mostly reining and gymkhana events. It wasn't long, however, before I announced that I wanted to learn to jump. Poor Harold would just look at me with his little half-smile as if to ask "where did I ever get this kid". I'm pretty sure that underneath it all he was having just as much fun as I was. Harold started giving me jumping lessons, and I couldn't get enough of it.

One Monday night at the auction, Harold bought a bay gelding that was headed for the "killers", the meat packing plant where horses that didn't have much use were slaughtered for dog food. We took him back to the barn that night in Harold's two-horse trailer. The horse was quite nervous, so Harold had me ride in the trailer with him, which made for two terrified passengers.

The following Saturday I was about to take out my first group on the trails, when Harold suggested I ride the new horse. The horse was not very attractive, he looked like he was constructed from spare parts, but Harold said ride him, so off we went. On the way back to the barn, we came upon a tree that had fallen across the trail. I detoured the group around it, but decided that since it was there I should jump it. The new horse jumped so high, he almost jumped me off. No hesitation, no fear, he just laid his ears back and charged the fallen tree. I had to contain my enthusiasm because Harold would not have liked me doing that in front of the customers. I rode back as if nothing had happened.

The next day I began bugging Harold to see if the new horse could jump. Finally, when he couldn't take it anymore, he agreed. I was not disappointed, and Harold seemed impressed as well. I had been saving to buy my own horse for some time. I was sure this was the one. I never could have done it without Harold. My father was not a big fan of my "wasting" so much time at the barn. Harold sold the horse to me for what he paid at the auction, and agreed to let me work off his board. I finally had my own horse. I paid $250 dollars for him. Since he was on his way to the "killers" when we got him, I named him Full Count, a baseball term meaning the batter is down to one last pitch. He turned out to be a really good little horse, not much by today's standards, but he always tried hard and gave his best. He won quite a few jumper classes in his career.

I never learned much theory about how horses jump from Harold or for that matter how to ride a jumper. I did get what I call my "cowboy education", however: how horses think, what they are afraid of, how to gain their confidence, and that there is a connection to a horse that separates horsemen from riders. I came to find out that not all riders are horsemen, and not all horsemen are riders, but the truly great ones are both. I also found out for the first time that life with horses is not always fun and games.

*   *   *   *

One Saturday while out on a trail ride, Rusty, Harold's favorite old school horse, fell and came up very lame on this right front leg. The veterinarian diagnosed it as a fractured scapular or shoulder blade and recommended putting Rusty down, but Harold wanted to try and save him. We devised a primitive sling in his stall to the take the weight off his legs. We brought him his hay and water, and we gave him almost no grain in the hope that he would not founder from lack of exercise. We hung a hay net in front of Rusty to keep him occupied and to keep some forage moving through his system. If he could live like that for a few weeks without colicing, he might recover, at least that was Harold's theory, and we both wanted to believe Rusty was going to be all right. I have no idea if the vet thought this hypothesis held any validity. Harold truly loved old Rusty, and so did I, so the idea seemed plausible at the time.

Rusty did pretty well for a while, but then he began to weaken. Deep inside, I expected it. Horses are meant to move. In nature they are foragers, always moving around, always alert, with three million years of evolution telling them to be ready to run at any sign of danger. It was humans that put them into stalls. Over the years I have found that if a horse is going to heal, he is usually going to do it naturally, out moving around.

One afternoon I arrived at the barn and found Harold in the tack room. He had tears in his eyes. He didn't have to say anything, I knew. Harold was as tough an old horseman as there was, but he loved those school horses, and Rusty was the best. Harold had a big favor to ask. He needed help burying Rusty in the back field. The two of us prepared for a job we both dreaded.

People who are not involved with horses don't really understand what it means when a horse dies. That is, they don't understand all the implications. A horse is a huge animal, as much as 1400 or 1500 pounds. When alive, they are majestic, graceful, and powerful. In death, they are a huge, lifeless mass. If they die inside the barn, getting them out can be a daunting task. The stall that we had set up for Rusty was intentionally adjacent to the back door. Harold had been able to get Rusty's carcass out to the back field with a chain and the pick-up truck. There is no dignified way to do it, and it had to be done right away, before rigor mortis set in. By the time I got there, all that remained was to bury him.

Harold was a good horseman and he worked hard, but the barn was not making him wealthy. He was barely keeping it afloat, and he had no money to hire a backhoe. Harold and I would have to dig the hole to bury old Rusty. We walked slowly out the rear door of the barn towards the field. Harold carried two shovels; I had a pick ax slung over my shoulder. It was August, brutally hot, and the flies around the barn and the manure pile, which was also in the back field, were overwhelming. I don't know how long it took us, but it seemed like forever. We dug right behind where Rusty was lying so we could lift his now-stiff legs and roll him over into the grave. Finally, it seemed deep enough. We both stopped digging and leaned on the handles of our shovels. I looked at Harold, his face was streaked with dirt; rivulets of sweat ran through it. Harold grabbed the hind legs, I took the front, and we lifted with all our strength. Rusty rolled right into the crater according to plan. By now all we wanted was to get this grisly job over with, and we both began furiously backfilling the hole. As it turned out our plan had a crucial flaw. When the dirt was all returned to the hole, those stiff legs that made it so easy to roll Rusty over, stuck straight out of the ground like a sick joke, I looked at Harold hoping for answers. We didn't know whether to laugh or cry, but since we had spent most of the afternoon crying, with our red eyes as proof, we laughed. After that momentary release, we knew that as ridiculous as it looked, we couldn't just leave him like that. Harold thought I had dealt with enough. He sent me home; then headed toward the barn to get his tools.

That day had a profound influence on my view of horses. Prior to Rusty dying, they seemed invincible. Big, and strong, and fast, they are a tribute to a combination of evolution and selective breeding. That day I realized how vulnerable horses really are, how dependent they are on us. Like it or not, we have become the stewards of these great creatures. They are no longer wild, no longer have the tools or instincts to survive without man, which hundreds of years of domestication have assured. I vowed that day to keep the trust. I would never take advantage of their giving nature, their kindness, and their desire to please us. I believe that with very few exceptions I have kept that trust. Those few exceptions make up the bulk of my regrets.

Young Entry Stable

The Broken Wheel Ranch remained my home-away-from-home well into my college years. I had chosen Stonehill College, located in the south shore town of Easton, Massachusetts, in large part because of its proximity to the stable. Each day after classes, some mornings before classes, and of course every weekend, I made my way to Sharon. After trying to balance school, the barn, and working in my father's restaurant, I didn't have much time for anything else.

One day during sophomore year I met a freshman who would change my life. Fran Cunning and I soon found out that we had a mutual interest and love of horses. We became friends instantly. Fran had been involved with horses all her life, her background being very different from mine. She had a number of wonderful horses, and over the years had been trained by some of the best trainers. Fran showed hunters and jumpers and studied under such trainers as Elaine Moore Moffat and Gordon Wright, the founding father of the American System, names she introduced me to. We talked a lot, and every Monday morning we found each other in the café to discuss how our horse shows went.

One morning over coffee, Fran was trying to figure out how she was going to be able to get to the horse show the next weekend. She planned to take two horses, but the person who usually helped her was not going to be available and she needed a hand loading and unloading. She shipped them herself in a two-horse trailer. She could also use a hand during the show, because two horses do more than just double what needs to be done with one horse. I immediately volunteered my services, saying that I would be at her family farm in Medfield early Saturday morning.

As planned, I drove into the driveway at 5:45 AM. The next level of my education as a horseman had begun. The farm was called the 1678 Farm for the year that the house and barn were first built. I was awe struck. Everything was so beautiful and pristine. This was not exactly what I was accustomed to at Bellevue Riding Academy or the Broken Wheel Ranch.

Fran and I went to many horse shows together over the next three years, and our friendship grew. After I graduated and Fran was a senior, we both realized that there was no one else we would rather be with, so we began dating. The next year, 1968, we were married.

Fran & I continued teaching school and competing as amateurs. Under American Horse Shows Association rules at the time, the only paid position involving horses that we could accept was as riding camp instructors. Thus began two wonderful summers at what was the best known of the Vermont riding camps, Teela-Wooket Camp in Roxbury. Over the years, the number of lifelong horse people that I met who started out at Teela-Wooket Camp is staggering.

The camp's riding director was an elderly Austrian horseman named Captain T. Fred "Cappy" Marsman. Cappy was the first person I knew who featured dressage as a discipline of choice. In 1969 not many Americans knew much about dressage, which was barely on the radar as a riding activity. Certainly, very few could have foreseen the level of interest that exists today. Although it was fairly well known among the staff at Teela-Wooket that some of Cappy's dressage riding was as a performer in the circus, he certainly knew more about dressage than anyone else at camp. That is, with the exception of Major Mike Antoniewicz, another instructor, who judged the dressage phase of the Olympic three-day event in 1936. (that's right, Major Mike judged the Olympic Games in Berlin during Hitler's regime). Meeting and becoming close friends with Major Mike was an unexpected bonus of our two summers at Teela-Wooket.

I wish we had known Cappy in his prime, but by the time we got to Teela-Wooket, he was definitely winding down his career. He had been the director of riding at camp for many years, and now he spent most of his time in his cabin. When he did venture out, he drove around in his mammoth vintage Cadillac, passing each of the rings where lessons were being taught, rolling down the window and hollering out in his heavy Austrian accent, "leg, leg, ya goot". Then he would move on to the next ring. Even if Cappy was no longer the trainer that he once was, you had to like him. He was personable and funny, and told wonderfully embellished stories about the old days. He could keep a room full of people entertained for hours, a talent that kept him in the director's position while Major Mike remained just an instructor. Major Mike, being the ultimate soldier, never complained.

Major Mike, a wonderful man with an incredible international resume, was, next to Fran, the greatest influence on my theories and beliefs regarding horses, riding and teaching. He had been the captain of the Polish riding team, back when the Poles were among the best in the world. He had ridden in four Olympic Games. In 1928, he won team medals in both the three-day event, (at that time it was called the military event) and grand prix show jumping, the first to have won a medal in both. Mexico's General Humberto Mariles repeated the feat in 1948. Jim Day of Canada was the last to attempt medaling in both disciplines in 1976.

When Major Mike judged the Olympic Games in Berlin in 1936, Hitler did his best to influence the judges by wining and dining them in the days before the games. Mike told a chilling story of being required to have dinner with Herman Goering. Just before the games began, all of the judges were "invited" to a meeting to be introduced to the Fuhrer himself. Tensions with Poland were already heightened, and Major Mike was not exactly a fan of Hitler. When Mike's turn came to be presented, he snapped to attention, but refused to salute the Fuhrer. Not long after those Olympics, Germany invaded Poland and Major Mike paid a high price for that act of defiance. He was one of the first arrested by the invading German army and spent five years in a prisoner of war camp. During that time he learned over a hundred different versions of solitaire. Quiet evenings in Vermont, he played them often, and tried unsuccessfully to teach them to us.

Major Mike came to this country after the war, and by the time we met him in 1969, he was semi-retired. He coached a few clients in Virginia, and taught at Teela-Wooket in the summer. He was in his early 80s at the time, but what he lacked in youth, he more than made up for with his enthusiasm. His message was simple – there are no short-cuts in training horses. His mantra was "be patient, be kind, be patient, be firm, and be patient". Major Mike became a tremendous influence in both our lives. It was his work ethic, his step-by-step approach, and his many confidence-building exercises that stayed with Fran and me. As a horseman, he had studied at a time when almost all Nations Cup teams were military, and he refused to accept the hurry-up world of capitalism. He would never allow the pressure of making a sale or keeping a client happy influence what he did with a horse. His training system was methodical, based on repetition, reward and a complete understanding of horses. It was also very non-commercial. Anytime I used any sort of "quick fix", I got a reminder.

If I put a martingale on a high-headed horse, or used a bit more severe than a snaffle, there would be Mike, at attention, with his perfectly groomed mustache inches from my face. "Joe, this is American instant coffee" he would pronounce, then turn on his heels and march off.

When we left Teela-Wooket to start our own summer program, Major Mike came with us. After watching Fran's lesson one of our last days at Teela-Wooket, Mike put his arm around her as they walked back up the hill that led away from the rings. "Fran", he said, "you are very good teacher, I will make you better". Major Mike died some years ago, well into his 90s, and yes, he did make us better teachers.

Although we met friends at Teela-Wooket Camp who have remained part of our lives to this day, the camp itself was on the down side of a long and successful run. The heyday of the all-around camp was going the way of the resort in the movie "*Dirty Dancing*". Children and their parents no longer wanted a camp with an hour of tennis, an hour of archery, and an hour of riding and so on throughout the day. They were more interested in becoming proficient at one thing. They wanted a tennis camp, a swimming camp or a riding camp, with skilled coaches and plenty of practice time. There was no mechanism at Teela-Wooket for that. A number of parents who were discouraged by the lack of progress their daughters were making in their riding approached Fran and me and suggested we start our own camp that focused on riding and horsemanship. With this kind of encouragement, we decided to do just that.

Starting our own riding camp sounded great. We were both school teachers, educators, who certainly would be up to the challenge of having a small summer camp. We had been married two years - I was twenty-five, Fran was twenty-four - and with the courage provided by youth, ignorance, and nothing to lose, we arranged to lease a farm in Royalton, Vermont about fifteen miles from Teela-Wooket.

I don't even remember how the Royalton connection happened, but the farm was owned by a very successful New York City attorney, who used the farm as a ski lodge in the winter, and who liked the idea of a summer use. He wanted to supply the cook and all the food supplies, so that was all figured into our price sheet. We printed up a two-page brochure, mailed it out, and advertised in "*The Chronicle of the Horse*", the sport's most popular weekly periodical. Miraculously, six sets of otherwise intelligent parents thought, "This is a good idea. I think we will send our teenage daughter off to Vermont with these two twenty-year-olds, who have no track record and have never been in business in their lives". It still amazes me. Fran and I named our new venture Young Entry Stable. A young entry is a first year hound in the world of fox hunting, and we thought the analogy was appropriate, this was our first year of business, and we were teaching young riders.

Less than two months before the start of our first summer program, we received a letter that almost ended it before it began, the owner of the farm was raising all the rental prices by a third. We were on a shoestring budget as it was, this was a deal-breaker. I was furious. I put on my best suit, (actually it was my only suit, if I recall) and got on the next train to New York City to tell this "big-shot lawyer" that he was not going to sabotage us.

I will never forget the feeling of walking, unannounced, into one of these high-rise Madison Avenue offices. The woodwork was all mahogany, with priceless works of art on the walls. The hardwood floors showcased the plush oriental rugs. The receptionist reminded me of my sixth grade teacher, Sister Daroma, who was really mean. I was totally intimidated, and I suppose that's the point of those offices, to give the lawyers the edge. To his credit, "Mr. Big Shot Lawyer" did agree to see me, but of course I was no match for his legal shenanigans and his experience. I left with nothing except a harsh life lesson.

When I got home, Fran and I decided the only thing we could do was to phone the six sets of parents who had put their trust in us and call the whole thing off. The deposits we had taken had been mostly spent on preparation, so calling it quits would be financially difficult for two young school teachers trying to start a business, but going forward would be a disaster. Fortunately, the first call we made was to the Heck family in Greenwich, Connecticut, whose daughter Debbie was our student at Teela-Wooket. The Hecks were really nice, kind people, so we decided they would be the easiest ones to call. We figured they wouldn't be too furious when they heard the news. That was an understatement. Mrs. Heck immediately offered an alternative. Her employer had recently become involved in a very large horse farm in Randolph, Vermont called the Green Mountain Stock Farm. Mrs. Heck interceded on our behalf, and it became our summer home.

I believe things happen for a reason. The Green Mountain Stock Farm was absolutely perfect for our purposes, much more appropriate for a camp than the farm that we lost. The farm is a magnificent twelve hundred acre tract of land just off Interstate 89 in Randolph, the geographic center of the state. It was originally built by Cornelius Knight, the founder of "Fruit of the Loom" underwear. We became familiar with the stories of how, in the eighteen hundreds, Mr. Knight would drive his buggy, and of course his prize Morgan horses from his farm in Providence, Rhode Island to his summer residence at the Green Mountain Stock Farm.

Our portion of the farm consisted of a barn, a riding ring, a few turn-out paddocks, and an old farm house. The stable was well built, although the stalls were somewhat small for the size horses we use for jumping (they were constructed for smaller and chunky, almost pony-sized Morgans). Otherwise, however, the barn was very serviceable. It had a wide center aisle. The stalls were built of solid maple, with bars on the front so the horses could look out. Each stall had a window at the rear that allowed ventilation and fresh air. At one end was a tack room with saddle and bridle racks.

Year one of Young Entry Stable's summer program (or YES as it became known) was a huge success by any measure. The teaching and learning environment was perfect. We had a captive audience of very motivated students, and no parents. Each rider had to bring his or her own horse, and we provided a few extras of ours and a sales horse or two. We formed such special bonds with the students we had in those early years that we still are in touch with many of them.

Days began with a 6:00 A.M. wakeup. Horsemanship was the emphasis, not just riding, so the kids themselves did all the work with the horses. The stable had to be cleaned and ready for inspection before breakfast. We had two formal lessons each day, plus a stable management lesson, and free riding time. A favorite activity was to ride bareback to the river and play around while the ice-cold water cascaded over the horse's tired legs. On weekends, we traveled to the local Vermont horse shows to find out how much we had learned.

The second year we had twelve "campers" (although we never referred to YES as a camp, our riders jokingly referred to themselves as "campers"). The third year we had eighteen riders, then twenty-eight. However, that was too many. Fran and I settled on a maximum of eighteen, and we stayed with that number for as long as we continued the summer program. The result was that eighteen became very exclusive. Over the winter we would interview numerous applicants, but since returning riders were given preference, there were usually only a few spaces to fill.

Early on the morning of February 1, 1973 we received a call that there had been a fire during the night at The Stock Farm. Only the small indoor ring and the adjoining barn had been destroyed. None of the area that we used had caught fire, but two volunteer fire fighters had been killed battling the flames when the roof of the indoor arena collapsed. Wild rumors had started to circulate that the fire might have been purposely set for insurance reasons. Some townspeople were very angry, and Fran and I decided that we should go elsewhere for awhile. The rumors were totally fabricated. The owners of that farm loved every inch of it, and financially would have no reason to do something like that. The truth came out eventually, when it was discovered that the fire was started by two young boys smoking in the loft.

While at GMSF we found Vermonters to be a very special group of people, who have tremendous pride in their way of life. They work hard, say little, pay their bills, and expect you to do the same. Outsiders have to prove themselves, and we were no exception, we were "flatlanders" after all.

Our first four years at the Stock Farm were a good start; we built solid relationships with many of the local vendors and businesses. One was a man named Skip Washer, or Skip "Washa" as he pronounced it in his very thick Vermont accent. We had been purchasing all our hay and stall bedding from Skip

We found our new temporary home (we returned to GMSF two summers later) at Ryder Brook Stables in Morrisville, we asked Skip to continue providing our hay and bedding. That spring as we prepared for our move to Vermont, Fran was pregnant with our first child. Since I was still teaching school, Fran and Pat Hite, our assistant at the time, headed to Vermont to get Ryder Brook ready for the season.

Fran called that night, she was as close to hysterical as I have ever heard her. The barn had been rented for the winter, but whoever had rented it had not cleaned a stall for the entire time. The stalls were literally two feet deep in old manure, and the rest of the barn was not much better. It was uninhabitable. I tried unsuccessfully to calm Fran down. The best I could come up with was to call Skip Washer. "Well", said Skip, "I got a lota hay down, and got a good deal more to cut while the weather holds". After a short pause he added, "I'll see what I can do. You tell Mrs. Fran not to worry".

That night Fran awoke to the roar of heavy equipment pulling onto the grounds. Six pair of headlights, three dump trucks, and three front end loaders paraded down the driveway toward the stable. It was after midnight, and it was Skip and his crew straight from haying all day and into the night. The next morning the barn was spotless. The stalls were cleaned and bedded and the aisles were swept. Skip and his men were long gone. Fran called him and thanked him profusely.

When I got to Vermont, we had Skip deliver a supply of hay and shavings. He presented me with a bill for one load of each. "I'd like to settle up for all you did the other night" I said. "Nope" replied Skip, "This is the only bill, the other night was for a friend in trouble. In Vermont that's different, that's not business." I was somehow shocked but not surprised. At that moment I felt like we belonged, that perhaps we weren't "flatlanders" anymore, at least not entirely.

Ponies

Our first daughter Annie was born in 1973. At that time we owned a small home on a dirt road in Medfield, Massachusetts and rented stable facilities in the area, including the barn at Fran's family's farm. A few years later, when we found out that we were going to have our second child, Julia, we knew it was time to make some major changes. The little house that we owned was barely big enough for the three of us, let alone a new baby. We managed to scrape together enough money for a down payment and purchased a ten-acre piece of property on Pine Street, also one of the last few dirt roads in Medfield. Finally, we had our own farm.

Although the stately Federal period farm house on the property had recently been renovated, the stable had been abandoned for some time and was desperately in need of repair. The main structure, the original livery stable for the town of Medfield, dated back to the sixteen hundreds. It had a huge loft with 12" x 12" hand-hewn hardwood timbers criss-crossing through it. Attached to the main barn was a newer, much lower structure that was constructed in maple sugar house style. On the other side of the main barn there was a workshop and three-car garage. Together they formed a U with a courtyard in the center.

The stable had great potential, but was nowhere near ready for occupancy when we bought it. The sugar house barn's entire floor had been removed or rotted out. There were no stalls still standing any where on the property, and all the roofs leaked badly. I can't imagine how many hours I spent getting it ready to move into. Sometimes we worked until 1 A.M., and then we would be right back at it the next day. A friend of ours, Bruce Berman, who helped me with the project, worked night after night with me, and would never let me pay him – not that we could afford to at that point. I will always be indebted to him; I never could have done it without his help. When it was completed, we had a really beautiful 25 stall barn that we could be proud of.

*   *   *   *

The Wylde family lived just down the street, John and Seddon, and their two sons MacRae and Peter. Both boys had taken a few riding lessons with Fran when they were quite young, but my first real memory of Peter was on his chestnut pony named Carmel. She was a very sweet, honest pony, but without that little blond boy, she was a very average show pony. With Peter riding her, however, she won a great deal. Peter was being coached by a young trainer named Clem Russell. Eventually the family sold Carmel and bought a "fancy" pony, but one with a reputation as a "stopper". The theory was that Peter would be able to turn it around and make the pony into a legitimate contender.

The pony division at major horse shows is usually comprised of five classes. The model, in which the rider-less pony is posed only in a bridle, then judged on its conformation; the under saddle, where all the ponies in the division walk, trot and canter in a group and are judged on how well they move; and three or four jumping classes. It becomes very difficult to be champion of the division if your pony does not place well in the model and under saddle. Peter's new pony could win both the model and under saddle, but would stop in the jumping classes, so if that could be corrected, he could be a great pony.

Peter gave the pony a wonderful ride, but some horses and ponies are just not meant for showing. Some have a real competitive side to their nature. They can sense that it is a competition and they really rise to the occasion. Not this pony, however, he galloped along, having a beautiful round, and then as he approached a jump he would grind to a halt and refuse to go any closer. Peter was around twelve at this time, and tough as he is, it took its toll, and Peter lost confidence. Fortunately, Clem and Wyldes realized the experiment was a mistake and got rid of the pony. They ended up donating it to a school as a flat lesson pony, which was a perfect fit.

Their next purchase was the polar opposite. It was a large green pony. A "green" horse or pony in horse show terms means inexperienced, usually in its first year of competition. "Large" is an official size designation indicating that a pony is taller than 13.2 hands high, but less than 14.2 hands. The pony was a bright chestnut color. He was so well built that he looked like a horse in pony clothes. Peter named him "Devil's River" after the river that ran past his grandparent's home in Canada. "Devil" was a fresh start, but considerable damage had been done to Peter's young confidence.

It was at this time that the luckiest thing in our careers happened to Fran and me – Clem Russell decided to give up training, and go back to college. I don't really know what became of him, but I hope it was all good. When Seddon and John Wylde asked if we would train Peter, Fran and I had all we could do not to look like blithering idiots. Everyone knew his potential. Peter and his family lived just a short walk from our barn. Peter kept his pony at home and cared for it himself. He could hack down the dirt road to our farm after school in just a few minutes.

It was initially decided that I would teach Peter. The next day Peter rode to the barn on his pony for his first lesson. This was my first time seeing Peter in a student \ teacher setting; it was also my first introduction to Devil as well. It is very different to train a rider and horse or pony than to just observe them in competition. It was clear from the first few seconds that we had some damage to undo. Peter, Devil, and I walked out to the field (we didn't have much of a ring at the time, just a big field with jumps in it).

I had Peter trot in a circle around me. Of course, since Peter took care of Devil himself, he also tacked the pony up himself. He had Devil trussed up like a chicken ready for roasting. Devil was wearing a tight martingale, draw reins, and a double twisted wire bit. These are all pieces of equipment that you would use to stop a runaway, but usually only one item at a time, not all at once. Devil, however, appeared to be anything but a runaway. He was trotting around me in a circle and although he did not look particularly happy, he was certainly not trying to run away

I knew what was going on in Peter's head. I had ridden my share of stoppers. We had to come to grips with his fear and start building some confidence and trust. I asked Peter to ride into the middle and talk to me. I explained what I was doing and why and asked him to trust me. I sent him and Devil into our stable. I told him to take all that gear off and borrow a simple snaffle from our tack room. A snaffle, the mildest bit you can use, consists of two pieces of round metal jointed in the middle and connected at the ends to rings. The rings are where the reins and bridle attach. Peter returned to the field with the equipment that I asked for and we began the lesson again. Devil responded as I had hoped. His head came down, his stride got longer, and his ears went up. He was much happier. From that day on, he never went in anything but a plain snaffle and no martingale.

Once Peter's confidence returned there seemed to be no limits to his talent and to his enthusiasm. Fran and I really had a lot of fun with the two of them. Devil was such an athlete. He never seemed like a pony. He moved like a horse, he jumped like a horse, and most importantly he thought like a horse. Devil was classic in his looks. He was a bright chestnut and his coat glistened. Peter was religious about his exercise routine, so his muscles rippled under his magnificent coat. It was his eye; however, that was the most beautiful. They say that the eye is the gateway to the soul; in horses this is even more true. I have never trained an exceptional horse that did not have a really kind eye, and Devil was no different. His eye was big, dark brown and soft. You could see his kindness in it. Devil was a giver, as all good horses are, and the story of his giving was right there in that eye.

Peter was a fantastic student. He absorbed everything like a sponge. His physical skills as a rider were different from most kids that age. He could do things on a horse that came very naturally for him, but that the others could not do with any amount of practice. Finding a distance (to jump from) was never an issue, it was a case of which distance he wanted to choose. He and Devil were one unit, thinking as one, working as one.

Even at his age, he was so coordinated that he could imitate all the top professional riders. He could make himself ride exactly in their style. Kevin Bacon was his favorite, an Australian who would throw his legs back as he cleared the jump and fly out of the saddle. He also perfected the styles of many others, such as George Morris, Buddy Brown, Rodney Jenkins, and even Leslie Burr. He would put on a show for us, and we would roll around on the ground laughing.

When it came to competition, however, Peter was very different. He was able to focus at a really young age. There was no joking around when he was "in the ring". He always maintained a wonderful and unusual combination of total focus and concentration with free wheeling and riotous fun.

Peter and "Devil's River", and another Championship.
Photo courtesy of the author.

Devil and Peter had a great first year together. They were champion at many of the best East Coast horse shows: Farmington, Ox Ridge, Saratoga, Fairfield, and many others. The culmination of the year came with Peter riding Devil to the 1979 Large Pony Hunter championship at the very prestigious Washington International Horse Show, one of the three fall indoor shows (the other two were the Pennsylvania National, and The National at Madison Square Garden in New York). You had to qualify for these three shows by accumulating points during the year, and when you made it there, you faced the best from all across the country. The Garden did not offer a pony division at that time, so for Peter and Devil, Washington was as challenging as it got.

The stake class, the last and most prestigious of the division, as well as the one with the most prize money, was so typical of the pair, and especially of Peter. As in most hunter classes, this one consisted of 9 or 10 jumping efforts. The last jump of the course was a single oxer at the end of a long diagonal approach. This is a very common way to end a hunter course, and often causes its share of problems because riders, especially young ones, have far too much time to think about what they should be doing. It is especially difficult if a young rider has had a good round because they start to think "only one more jump and I've got it" and that is almost a sure set up for a "miss".

Devil and Peter were having a terrific round, "nailing it" as we say, and were rounding the end of the giant arena heading for that last jump. Usually, in this situation, you would want your student to hold a nice easy canter across the diagonal until he could see where he wanted to "leave the ground" or take off, usually from three or four strides away, and then urge his pony forward. As Peter turned the corner, he shocked Fran and me, and everyone else in the arena, when he pressed Devil into a powerful gallop. It would have been a disaster for almost any other young rider, but Peter had "seen" that distance from ten or twelve strides away and just galloped right up to it. It gave me goose bumps. Any question of who would win the class was over in that instant. Peter and Devil got a tremendous round of applause from the crowd. Brian Flynn, a well known trainer and rider sitting near me, looked over and asked, "Did he see that? He didn't see that did he?" My heart still pounding, I confidently replied, "Oh yeah, he saw it". "Wow, he's special" Brian answered. We had only gotten a glimpse of how right he was.

We kept Devil another year, which was probably a mistake. Peter had grown dramatically over the two years and didn't really fit Devil correctly anymore. They struggled to find their balance and didn't have the same success as the previous year. With a lot of mixed emotions, we sold Devil at the end of the year. After the wonderful start that Peter had given him,

Devil went on to be an equally great pony for a number of families over the years that followed. The last ones to show him was a family from Texas named Ruff, their two daughters Tracy and Kelly both rode him. After his show days were over, the Ruffs retired Devil at their trainers beautiful farm in Virginia. Devil died there in 1996, well into his thirties. I was always grateful that The Ruff family and Jean Marie (Miller) Dunford took such wonderful care of him as he got older. Sometimes great show horses and ponies, like race horses, don't always get that respect once they can no longer perform. They must be special people, and I'm glad they got a special pony.

The Washington International Horse Show, 1979. Left to right: Peter (seated), Annie, Joe, Linda Perry and Fran. Photo courtesy of the author.

Native Surf

eter's success with Devil had attracted a lot of attention from other trainers. A great deal of that attention was unwanted, at least by Fran and me, as it was in the form of those trainers attempting to convince Peter and his parents that his career would benefit from a change to their stable and their training. A number of the major show stables "made a run" at getting him, but none of this got very far with the Wyldes. Although other barns had a lot to offer Peter in terms of wonderful horses to ride and a proven track record in developing outstanding riders, the Wyldes were loyal to us and comfortable that Peter's best interest was with us. Every year that passes, I appreciate their loyalty more; especially today, when there seems to be almost no loyalty at all left in the sport. I have no idea why they chose not to take advantage of all those offers, but I am eternally grateful that they didn't.

One well-known trainer approached the idea of having Peter ride for him differently, through us, and it ended up benefiting everyone. Walter J. "Jimmy" Lee, has trained some of the best hunters in the country for many years, and is one of the sport's most respected horse show judges. He is a tremendous horseman, and although we barely knew him at the time, he has become a longtime friend. One winter night we got a call from Jimmy, who said he had been watching Peter develop as a rider and was very impressed, then he took the time to congratulate us on the job we were doing with Peter. Jimmy said he had a number of quality young horses for sale and could use a good young rider for a couple of the summer months. He felt that Peter being seen in a different area of the country would help build his reputation and widen his experience. Most important to Fran and me, he said if we did not want this conversation to have taken place, it would not be mentioned again.

Our business had developed enough that we had very competitive riders and horses on the regional, New England level, but on the national scene we were not yet a blip on the screen (except for Peter and Devil of course). It made sense to us to give Peter some exposure in a different part of the country, but losing him for the summer would certainly be difficult. We had a meeting with the Wyldes and decided to accept Jimmy's offer. Soon after, Peter shipped off to Belcort Farm in Keswick, Virginia.

During Peter's stay in Virginia, Jimmy got a horse into his stable to sell on commission. His name was Native Surf, a grey Thoroughbred, that at one time had been a very good confirmation hunter. The great George Morris rode him during his glory years, and was champion at the indoor shows with him; Harrisburg, Washington and New York. By this time he was a little older, and was being shown in the Amateur-Owner hunter division with moderate success. Peter knew we were looking for an amateur horse for one of our customers, so we flew down to try him.

If you were commissioned to take photographs for a calendar of Virginia, Jimmy Lee's Belcort Farm would be an excellent place to start. Not that it is the biggest or the fanciest of the farms in that area, but it is just so classic Virginia. At the entrance are two imposing stone pillars that support a decorative wrought-iron gate that I am not sure actually closes. What seems like miles of freshly painted black four board fencing line the acres of paddocks framing magnificent Thoroughbred horses standing ankle deep in lush green grass. Jimmy's home on the farm looks like a country inn. The stable is workmanlike and pristine, and everything on the property is meticulously cared for.

We drove up the long winding driveway to meet Peter at the barn. Jimmy was away judging, so we had the facility to ourselves. Peter had Surf all groomed and cross-tied, in the Barn's center aisle. He looked magnificent. Peter must have worn out his grooming tools on him. Grey horses are very hard to get clean. They seem to relish rolling around in the worst mess they can find, and Surf was no exception. As we later found out, he seemed to get a kick out of seeing your expression when you found him in the morning. But on this day Peter had him so shiny you could almost see your reflection in his coat. Fran and I walked slowly around him, bending over occasionally to feel a tendon or pick up a foot. Surf was very gentlemanly throughout the entire inspection. He was getting older for certain, a couple of windpuffs, a little "over at the knee", but in all still had that classically sculpted body that had served him well when he competed in the Conformation division as a young horse. Eventually, we did purchase "Surf" for our client, and he headed north to live in Massachusetts.

Peter returned home at the end of August a better rider, and a more mature young man. He learned a lot, but was glad to be home. When we sold Devil's River the previous spring, we decided to wait until after Peter got back from Virginia to look for a horse for him. Finding Peter a horse was something we all looked forward to, but it was a job that turned out to be a lot harder than we had imagined.

The horse we bought for Peter would have to be a special one if he was going to reach his great potential. The plan was to buy a quality horse that was still fairly green, because Peter was still young enough to give the horse the experience it would need to be a contender. He also had the patience that it takes to bring a horse along. Very few junior riders have that kind of patience, they require instant gratification, but we thought Peter could handle it. There was no real hurry, because Peter had plenty of horses at the barn and catch rides from other stables to keep him busy.

During the year that we tried horses for Peter, Native Surf became available for sale. In order to help get him sold, Surf's owner let Peter take him to some horse shows. The combination was special right from the start. The picture of this beautiful grey Thoroughbred with this handsome blonde boy was hard to resist. They started to win, and win a lot. That year they qualified for the New England Finals, the AHSA Medal and the ASPCA Maclay. Peter and Surf were starting to get noticed. They won the New England Finals in September, 1981. It was a nice win, but the New Englands were not yet the important finals that they are today. When we got to the national finals that year, we found out that maybe we weren't yet ready for prime time. By the following year, we would be ready. That would be the year we would make our mark. That year Peter would be a contender.

The author and Peter at the Winter Equestrian Festival. Photo courtesy of the author.

1980 was the last year of our summer program in Vermont. Although we hoped to return someday, the Vermont one-day summer shows were no longer enough to keep the riders whom we were now attracting interested and challenged (the Vermont Summer Festival was not yet in existence). A number of the riders who were with us in the summer no longer wanted to leave us the rest of the year, so Young Entry became a year-round show barn from Massachusetts instead of a summer program in Vermont.

The other problem posed by summers was what to do with Peter. Young Entry Summer Program was a resident program for girls. Fran and I knew we couldn't keep leaving Peter for eight weeks and expect to find him there when we returned. Our desire to keep him in the fold ranked high on the list of reasons for not continuing our summers in Vermont. We were moving forward, but it was very sad in many ways, Young Entry Summer Program had been very good to us.

*   *   *   *

Peter was growing up. He started with us as a little boy who would hack his pony down the winding dirt road from his home to our barn for lessons, and now was maturing into a young man. Peter took great pride in being part of Young Entry, and was involved in every aspect of the operation. He also became a big part of our family. He spent hours at the barn every day, after school, weekends, vacations - any available time he had was spent at the stable. And, it usually did not end when the workday ended. Peter would often hang out at our house, or babysit the girls if Fran and I went out for a night. When he did babysit, the house would be in shambles when we returned, showing the remnants of pillow fights and fort-building. The girls both adored him, however, and always wanted to know when we were going out again so Peter could come over and babysit. He made everything fun.

At one point when Fran and I decided we needed a short vacation, Peter convinced us he could take care of everything at the barn. While we had no doubt the horses would be perfectly taken care of, his aptitude for getting into mischief had us a little concerned. We shipped the girls off to their grandparents and headed out for a few days in Nova Scotia, our first vacation in quite a while. While we were gone, Peter decided he and the other juniors at the barn should decorate the house for our return. They scoured the neighborhood and surrounding area for all the ugliest lawn decorations they could find to "borrow". We returned after dark one evening to find dozens of massive lawn ornaments, fountains, imitation swimming pools, pink flamingos, and anything else you might imagine set up on our lawn. For the coup de grace, they were all outlined in Christmas lights. I must admit, after the initial shock, the prank was hilarious. The next day was spent sneaking around in our pick-up truck attempting to locate the rightful owners of these hideous ornaments and returning them without detection.

When it came to the barn and the horses, as far as Peter was concerned, this was his barn, and these were his horses. He completely organized everything. He would plan for the shows, make lists and more lists and get every thing ready to go. He was equally good about involving all the other kids and making them feel a part of the program as well. Everyone had his or her part to play, and Peter was the conductor.

When Peter turned sixteen, we were about to go to the prestigious Hampton Classic Horse Show. We needed him to drive one of the cars so we could get everyone and everything to Long Island. Peter was scheduled for his driver's test, but not until after we had to leave, and we had no backup plan if he didn't pass his test. I called a friend from the old neighborhood who worked for the Department of Motor Vehicles, he gave the driving tests at a certain location once a week. We arranged for Peter to take his driving test, and my friend (who shall remain nameless) promised me that unless Peter was a total disaster he would make sure that Peter passed. Peter had been driving the tractors and pick up trucks around the farm for years, I knew he could drive, but I just wanted to make sure he would get his license on time to drive to South Hampton.

I was not available to go with Peter for his test, so Fran did. Fran and Peter are not the best combination for serious times like driver tests. They tend to find everything in such situations funny. For the most part the testing went very well. Peter was in the front seat with my friend the inspector, and Fran, Peter's sponsor, was alone in the backseat. Back at the DMV, as the test was nearing a conclusion, the inspector instructed Peter to parallel-park the vehicle by pulling along side the next car and backing into the space. This is the part that most young drivers dread, and I knew Peter did. When the car came to a stop, Peter turned to look out the back window. As he did, his elbow hit the "on" switch for the windshield wipers and his hand hit the horn. Picture that with the wipers going full speed and the horn blowing, he had turned and was looking right into Fran's face. The two of them completely lost it. They laughed until tears rolled down their faces. I'm sure by now my inspector friend was regretting helping me out. He suggested perhaps he could park the vehicle himself and sent Peter and Fran on their way. Peter got his license and drove to Long Island without once having to parallel-park.

The 1982 Medal Finals
The Big Chip

A s the 1982 show season approached, Peter was sixteen years old. He had been very successful with Devil in the pony division and in piloting the many catch rides he was being offered in the hunter ring. He was winning his share of classes in the equitation at the major shows, but up to this point he had not been a contender at the finals; the two year end national championships for junior riders. Chronologically, the first one is the USEF Hunter Seat Medal held in mid-October at the Pennsylvania National in Harrisburg, Pa., (at the time it was called the American Horse Shows Association Medal,) the second was the better known ASPCA Maclay Finals held in early November at New York City's Madison Square Garden. Junior riders from all over the United States compete to qualify for these two major events. (A third final sponsored by the United States Equestrian Team in Gladstone New Jersey was just getting started and had not yet reached the status of the other two).

Qualifying requirements have changed through the years, but during that time period, a junior rider had to win three Medals and three Maclays to qualify for the Finals. Unfortunately, second did not count for anything and that was cause for a great deal of frustration for many young riders.

The equitation division is unique to the United States (and Canada), and the same is true of the hunter division. In Europe and the rest of the world, a horse competes either as a jumper or in dressage. In hunter-seat equitation, the rider is being judged on position, style, and how he or she affects the horse. The judge rewards good form as it relates to function. It is a subjective form of judging, similar to ice skating or gymnastics.

The difference is that in equitation you cannot be successful without an equally talented horse. A rider must not only demonstrate how well he rides, but also how well he has trained his horse. In international competition the equitation division has resulted in the United States producing a seemingly endless supply of riders with classic style. We don't always have the best horses in the world, and our riders may not always be as battle-tested at the international level as the Europeans, but we always ride with great style.

The previous year, in the autumn of 1981, Peter had won the New England Equitation Championship held that year in Hamilton, Massachusetts. Having gained a great deal of confidence from that success, we went to the finals with great hopes, only to be disappointed by Peter and Surf having an uncharacteristically horrible round. One reason that we had such high expectations was that one of the two Maclay judges was Michael O. Page, who had judged the New England Finals. We could not believe Peter rode so poorly, and neither could Peter. He chipped so many times during his round at the Maclay finals that the whole next year when he chipped at home, we all sang, "I love New York". We were all determined not to have a repeat. Peter was impressive qualifying, winning all three of his classes at major shows and against top competition. This was Peter's next to last year as a junior, and it was time to "take our shot" at competing for a ribbon. With almost 300 other juniors on the same mission, however, that would be easier said than done.

We arrived at the 1982 Medal Finals with a good deal of confidence that grew out of the success we had during the year. Peter and Surf had shown themselves to be solid contenders.

Surf seemed particularly nervous on Saturday during the schooling hunter class that gives the opportunity to get into the ring, get a feel for the footing, let the horses see the inside of the coliseum, and get out some of the "butterflies". It was not terribly unusual for Surf to be nervous the first time in the ring, but since this was a national championship, we naturally fretted a little more over each detail. There are many things at a competition that as a trainer you can't control, and it's a waste of time and effort to worry about them, but we knew going a little slower with Surf that day would pay dividends so we gave him all the time he needed to relax, and he finally did.

Medal day, Sunday, begins with a course walk at 6:00 A.M.. If you are good enough and lucky enough to contend for a ribbon, the class likely will be completed about 6:00 P.M., twelve hours later. It is a grueling day in a Darwinian sense; only the strong survive. Fran and I had not yet had a ribbon-winner at the finals, and like every year, we were hopeful that this would be the year.

We had trained some very good riders, but a ribbon at Harrisburg or New York is a fragile combination of rider skill, a quality horse that is ready to compete at his highest level on that day, and a good measure of luck. In competition against other humans, an athlete has only to worry about him or herself and his equipment. In riding, the variables are multiplied. The horse is the biggest variable. Is he sound? Is he brave? How is he feeling today? Did he get any sleep last night with all the noise in the show stable area? Most important, is he ready to compete? When the gate to the coliseum opens, will he meet the challenge or will he want to go back to the safety of his stall? The horse is not the only variable, though. What style do the judges prefer? Does the course play into our strengths or our weaknesses? There are plenty of things that can go wrong, and that all those variables line up on that one special day is the dream of every trainer and rider assembled at the national championship.

Fran and I were training three other riders besides Peter that day. The plan was for us all to meet at our stalls at 5:30 A.M.. The parents drew straws to see who would be the lucky one to drive the kids to meet us, and who would get a few more glorious minutes of sleep. Our head groom, Tracy Emmanuel, had been there for hours, and so had her assistant. Usually we preferred our riders to do their own work with their horses, but at the Finals we always brought some extra help because of the added stress and the time constraints that come with a national championship.

Every course asks a number of questions. It is a mathematical test, conceived by the course designer on paper and then constructed in the show ring out of brightly painted obstacles. Each jump in the ring is related to the rest of the course in some way. There are questions being asked all the way around. They are questions of pace and direction. There are places where a rider must lengthen his horses stride and places where he must shorten it. The winner this day will make those adjustments without anyone being able to see it, especially the judges. While walking the course on foot, a rider, together with his or her trainer, attempts to discover what questions are being asked and to construct a "game plan" about how to answer those questions. Every horse and rider combination has strengths and weaknesses of course. When you walk, you hope that the questions the course asks play to your strengths. If not, you must be that much stronger and tougher, or your day is apt to end very early.

Peter had no glaring weaknesses as a rider. He would sometimes flap his elbows when he wanted to get going in what we jokingly called "the Peter Wylde chicken flap", but that was fairly minor. On the other hand, his strengths were many. He had a wonderful "feel" for pace and for his horse, an accurate "eye" (meaning that he always knew where he wanted to leave the ground), and no fear – he was always relaxed on a horse. But Peter's greatest quality as a rider is that he is a competitor. He is focused and mentally tough, and he will rarely make mental mistakes that will let you beat him. In addition, he was used to riding so many horses each day at the barn and having so many "catch rides" at shows, that if the judges asked riders to change horses as a test of the top riders, as they often do at the finals, he had a significant advantage.

Surf had his strengths as well. He had the ability to make a tight take-off to a jump look correct. He had such quick front legs that he was never in jeopardy of having a bad jump at a close or deep distance. Surf was also very brave. He was not afraid of the crowd, the jumps, or other horses. He never got "spooky" from the tension of a big show or a new place. Although Surf did not get "spooky", he could become tense, which he showed by getting strong. He would pull on the reins, and he could pull hard. He also would get very stiff on his right side, so stiff that you might have thought you were riding an oak plank. Any course with a number of difficult right hand turns was an increased challenge for us but Peter had become very adept at masking Surf's weaknesses.

The course seemed fair and it didn't appear that any of our horses or riders would be over faced. Trainers often have a variety of students with us when we arrive at the Finals. Sometimes we are fortunate enough to bring an experienced contender like Peter, other times it's a very nervous first timer. Most often, we are training an assortment of experience and skill levels. The plan for the day is rarely the same for any two riders. It is a gut-wrenching feeling to walk that course early in the morning and know one of your kids is in trouble. There is always the tension of waiting to see if your riders are up to the challenge, of feeling that they are well prepared and hoping they will show it on this big day, but you never want to feel that one of your riders is in over his or her head. A course can be a stretch because you don't improve unless you stretch, but not in over a rider's head.

The course had about 15 or 16 jumping efforts, which is about normal. It began with a long four-stride line, also very typical. The judges and course designers at the finals often start the course with a long first line to see who is star-struck and who came to play. Since your horse never gets to see the course until he has to jump it, the job of putting the plan together belongs to the rider and trainer. They spend a great deal of time learning how to walk the lines; the distances between jumps on a course. The idea is to figure out how to make four of your strides equal to one cantering stride of your horse. Then, you learn to factor in a half-stride for take off and landing, and you can put a plan together to help you and your horse negotiate the course safely and smoothly. Starting the course with a long first line immediately separates the contenders from the pretenders. If you're not riding forward from stride one, you're in trouble. If you add in that extra short stride, you make the judge's work easy because you're out. It's a long way around the next fourteen jumps, if you chip at the second fence.

Horse show jumps can be broadly divided into two types; verticals and oxers. Verticals, which have only one set of uprights, do not have width, only height. Oxers most often have two pairs of uprights or standards, but may have three. They have both height and width. Both types of jumps can be made to look very unique by what the course designer uses to fill them in with. They use rails, and walls painted to look like brick or field- stone. They use gates and planks and flowers and shrubs, and when finished a talented course designer has created at the very least an interesting and attractive mathematical puzzle and possibly a work of art.

I believe the job of the course designer is the most crucial at the Finals. The challenge is to make the course difficult enough to separate the best junior riders in the country, without making it dangerous. A few years later I would have this put into perspective by a Canadian course designer friend named Robert Jolicour. We were officiating at a show in California, I was judging, and Robert was the course designer. After the show ended one day, I was unhappy about the way one of my classes had gone - I just didn't feel good about the way it was pinned. Robert asked what was bothering me, so I told him. "Don't be rrrediculous" he said in his charming French-Canadian accent. "You make a mistake, someone gets the wrrrong color rrribbon, I make a mistake and someone gets kilt". And although it sounded more like something a Scotsman wears than an accident, I got the point. The course designer has a tremendous responsibility. Robert was right, and I never forgot it.

On one side of the arena, was a triple combination, a series of jumps at a prescribed distance from one another, either one or two strides apart.

A double is two jumps, a triple is three, separated by a maximum of two strides. This particular triple was a two-stride followed by a one-stride, an oxer to another oxer and then to a vertical. The problem it presented was that the first two strides were long or "forward", a situation exacerbated by the oxers, and the second distance was short, made more difficult by the choice of a vertical. For Peter and Surf, the first two strides would be a little more difficult than the short one stride. As long as Peter "rode up to it" with enough pace and didn't slow down or "pick" his way to it, they should be fine. We all knew Surf would snap those lightning legs and make the vertical look perfect. "Just ride up to it, keep him balanced, and keep your leg on" I told Peter as we walked the triple. He nodded, and we moved on to the next line.

Peter's place in the starting order was somewhere near the middle of the roughly 280 qualifiers that had made their way to Harrisburg for the first round of the 1982 AHSA Medal Finals and between twenty and thirty of that group would eventually be good enough to make it past the first round. At regular intervals of around fifty, a standby list is announced. The list includes those still in contention to make the second round. It is often, but not always, in reverse order of standing. Anyone not on the list can return to the stable area, perhaps shed a few tears, unbraid the horse, change into street clothes, and then go back to the arena to watch, or go home. It was a scenario we were all too familiar with, and it made for a long ride home.

Harrisburg's warm-up ring in those days was outside, and as always it was a wild scene. Trainers attempt to recreate the course problems in the schooling area, but they have far fewer resources in terms of jumps and space. Jumps were set up every which way. Coolers and blankets were hung over the rails and folding chairs and barrels were used as jump fillers. Some riders were even jumping the fence that separated the schooling area into two halves. We did not school Peter and Surf over any of these unusual jumps. Our theory was to make courses so difficult at home that the show would seem to be easy. We were not big on last-minute heroics, which usually only unnerve the horse or rider or both. We warmed Surf up the way we always did - slowly. He seemed fine. Peter looked great. He was confident. One last vertical, we were ready.

When Peter and Surf were on deck, we gave him his final instructions. Fran and I moved to the spot where the trainers traditionally stood, a dozen steps up to a small platform area at the bottom of the first row of seats. The stands spread out to our left, and rose steeply behind us. The arena and all its newly painted jumps lay ominously in front of our little platform. The only thing separating us from the ring was the pipe railing of the giant coliseum. I wrung the top rail in my hands, like you would ring out a dish rag. My heart was pounding. I knew this was the closest we had ever come, maybe the closest we would ever come, to a chance at the championship. I glanced at Fran. She looked as cool as ever.

Fran is almost fanatical about preparation. She knows that her horse and rider are ready, so she has the power to focus on what has to be done and not get caught up in the emotion and excitement of the moment. She is a truly wonderful teacher. Her calm is picked up by the young riders. Staying calm is harder for an Italian, but I try my best because I know that is what our kids need.

As the previous horse and rider exited the far end of the arena, the in-gate opened, and Peter and Surf walked into it. The coliseum fell into total silence as it does when one of the favorites enters. "This is a good sign", I thought. I twisted the rail one last time, my knuckles whitened. Peter moved Surf off his left leg to get the bend that he needed, and then stepped into a left-lead canter. They "nailed" the first line, the long four. Half a dozen more jumps, and then the triple combination – two strides, then one; perfect! They were laying down a great trip as they rounded the turn to the last jump. They had been brilliant so far. I could feel my hands, slippery with sweat, slide as I gripped the rail.

Most trainers have a way of expressing to their rider and the crowd and the judges when they think their student's round was exceptionally good. I have a very loud whistle that I can start down low and then bring up the scale to an explosion of sound while I clap furiously. These displays don't really have any effect on the judges, but it adds to the excitement. It is a horse SHOW, after all.

Peter and Surf were approaching the last fence. Fran glanced at me, "Get ready to whistle, and make it loud", she whispered. The last fence was perfect. I wet my lips and let fly with as loud a whistle as I could muster. Fran was clapping wildly next to me. Suddenly, we realized the entire crowd was applauding and whistling. As Surf walked out the far end of the ring, Fran and I leapt down the stairs and ran to meet Peter.

At Harrisburg, the rider always enters at one end and exits at the other. To meet your student after their round, you must walk to the opposite end in the walkway under the coliseum seating. They emerge from a tunnel that leads away from the out-gate. Peter was smiling. Fran pointed out a few things that could have been better, but overall we were thrilled. Now came the agony of waiting for the standby list. There were about twenty more riders before we would learn whether the judges agreed that his was a round worth keeping. Through the years we had on occasion been disappointed for other riders. We tried not to let Peter see how nervous we were.

The standby orders are announced after a short break when the ring is dragged and watered for the next group of fifty riders. The instant the horse show announcer's voice is heard, everyone knows what is coming; either you are still in the fight or your day is over. Trainers, riders and parents are all prepared with pen and paper. Since the list is usually in reverse order, if your number is read near the end, the judges most likely have you near the top. However, if you are in the first few, especially if it is an early list, you are probably not going to make the second round, but for many the day is a success just to be mentioned for that brief time. To be able to say you made the standby at Harrisburg is an honor.

The countdown was ready to begin. The announcers voice rang through the arena; "We have the standby through the first 150 riders". "The following riders are asked to standby at this time; number 112, number 26, number 86." He completed the first 10; no Peter. That was bad news and good, because if he was in that group, he probably would not make the next round. But for two young trainers who had yet to make the list, we just wanted to be somewhere. We would all be devastated if that round wasn't good enough. Ten more numbers; no Peter, we were really getting worried but were trying to hide it from Peter. Then, in the middle of the last group, there it was. "Keep writing" I thought, how many more, how many ahead of us? One, two more numbers were announced. "Jesus" I said half to Fran, half to myself, "We're third". When the first round ended, and the dust cleared, three more riders had fought their way into the top ten ahead of us. We finished the first round in sixth place.

After a considerably longer break for the ring to be dragged and watered, and the course to be set, it was time for the twenty-eight riders and their trainers to walk the new course. It was approaching four o'clock in the afternoon, and everyone had been on the grounds since about five that morning. We were all exhausted, only the adrenalin that had kicked in with the thrill of making the next phase was keeping us going. Making the second round for the first time had forced the desire for sleep take a back seat for now. At 6:00 A.M. there were literally hundreds of riders and trainers in the ring; now there were just a handful of us. It was much easier to see the course and get to the jumps. Peter seemed very much under control, very focused

The course itself was considerably more difficult than the one in the morning, but still we thought, very rideable. The last line was a single oxer, then four strides to the triple combination, which had been reversed. Instead of being a long two strides followed by a short one stride, it was now a quiet one to a long two strides. As we finished our walk, Fran, Peter and I huddled to review it. We never tried to feed Peter too much information at the last minute. He did so many great things naturally; we didn't want to make him mechanical. We made sure we all agreed on the basic plan, and started to walk toward the in-gate. As we walked, I said to Peter, "Be careful with the triple - the two might get long - keep your leg there". Peter was pumped about being in the fray. (We often called him "Mr. Enthusiasm" because he was always so positive in his approach to riding. He never backed down or got negative). He smiled at us and said, "Don't worry; by the time we get here, we'll be cruising". He flashed a big grin. He was kidding with me, and I was glad he was so relaxed. This was the biggest moment of his career to this point, and he seemed totally relaxed and confident.

One by one, the riders returned to the ring for their second round. As always, they rode in reverse order, the twenty-eighth competitor returning first, and the higher ranked riders coming near the end. This procedure eventually builds pressure on those riding later in the class, but on the plus side, it allows them to see how the course is riding and how their plan is holding up.

Rider after rider made mistakes; the course was taking its toll. Some of the younger riders succumbed to their nerves; the more experienced ones weren't getting it done. As our turn grew nearer, no one had laid down a really good trip. Finally, the rider in front of us was on course, we were next. We had given Peter his final instructions a few minutes earlier. Peter always needed the last couple of minutes to be alone with his thoughts; to focus. Over time we found that approach to be the best with most of our riders. I never understood trainers barking instructions to their riders as they are walking into the ring. It probably is more trainer nervousness than educational. We said good luck, and returned to our "spot" on the rail. Again, I grabbed the rail and squeezed. I glanced to my left and noticed one of that era's most successful trainers, Paul Valliere, sitting next to us. I raised my eyebrows and nodded, as if to say, "Here goes". Paul smiled.

Peter and Surf entered the ring, and struck off at the canter. This was it. Line by line, he picked the course apart, answering all the questions the course designer had asked, "cruising" as he had promised. As he turned to meet the last line, you could hear a pin drop. I could feel my heart pounding. The oxer was perfect. Peter stayed in on the line to the triple and made the four strides ride easily. He jumped into the triple; one soft easy stride, then over the second element. He pressed Surf forward; they took one stride, then two. I wet my lips. What a round. Then the impossible happened. Just as Peter softened his back to leave the ground, Surf threw those "lightning legs" back down, and put in an extra stride. It was a disaster, a total disaster. Adding a stride in a combination is a major fault. In scoring terms, in that instant, he went from a 90 to a 55. We went from one jump away from leading the class to being completely out, with no chance for a ribbon. I squatted down on the cold concrete step behind me. I looked to my left. Paul was smiling. Not a mean smile, more like the knowing smile of some who's been there. "So ya think it's easy" he said. No, of course I never thought it would be easy, but we were soooo close.

Suddenly, I snapped my head up and looked at Fran. At the exact same time, we both said "Peter". We realized in that instant, as disappointed as we were, he must be devastated. We ran down the stairs, and headed to the end of the tunnel where Peter and Surf would emerge. "What will we say"? I asked Fran. She paused for a few seconds, looked up at me, and said, "I have no clue". In another instant, there he was, walking out of the tunnel on Surf. Fortunately, we didn't have to say anything. When Peter saw us, he broke into a big smile, swept his right arm across in front of his chest, and snapped his fingers. "Woops!" was all he said as his dismounted. He gave Surf a big pat and whispered "Sorry, boy", then with some urgency he asked; "Can you guys hold Surf for a second, Sandy goes next, I really want to watch her", and off he went. Sandy was his good friend, Sandy Nielsen, from Connecticut, who eventually won the medal that day. All I could think of at that moment was a quote by the great trainer Frances Rowe. When someone asked her who was the best rider she ever worked with, she answered "Conrad Homfeld, because he never held his mistakes against his horses".

We have always maintained that we learned as much or more from Peter as he ever learned from us. I sure learned a lot that day. Peter never let a bad round or a mistake affect his next round. When a class is over, it is history. You learn what you can from a mistake, and move on. I have found this to be a strength of most really good riders; it is certainly one of Peter's, and a major reason why two weeks later he was able to completely dominate the next Final.

The Garden

The National Horse Show began in 1883, and for most of its 123 years it resided at the world's most famous sports arena; Madison Square Garden in New York City. Although its official name was The National Horse Show, everyone connected with horses just called it "The Garden". Traditionally, The National was the official opening of the Manhattan social calendar. In the nineteen seventies and eighties, although a tuxedo was no longer mandatory, men still didn't show up on weekends without a coat and tie, and ladies wore appropriate evening attire. Judges, wore formal dress. Trainers were also expected to look the part; sport coat and tie for men, and a skirt or pant suit for the ladies. Evening performances on weekend were totally sold out. There was no slipping in for free if you were a trainer or an exhibitor, as you can at any other horse show; if you didn't have a ticket, you didn't get in. The Maclay Finals would often have as many as 10,000 spectators in the stands in its heyday. The National was also one of the few remaining multi-breed shows. Spectators would be treated to Saddlebreds and hackneys, hunters and jumpers, and an endless array of demonstrations from dressage to Western riding. The jumpers included international teams from all over the world. In those days it was rare to see our U.S. Equestrian Team compete, so it was always a treat to see the flags from all the competing nations draping the end of the arena, and our Team members wearing their formal scarlet coats.

As for what "The Garden" meant to the horse world as a business, its impact was immeasurable. Every young child who loved horses wanted someday to "ride at the Garden". No matter how little any loving grandparent knew about horses and horse shows, they knew what competing at Madison Square

Garden meant. The winter horse show circuits were just getting started at that time, and the first week in November was made even more special because it was the last show until Spring. Excitement built to a crescendo as the days left to qualify ticked away. Without a doubt, "The Garden" was the single most important factor in the meteoric rise in the popularity of riding over the past thirty years, especially the discipline called hunter-seat equitation.

For many years, the driving force behind "The Garden" was Mrs. Kenneth Wheeler. She certainly was its driving force for the time that we were fortunate enough to be exhibitors. Her full name was Sallie Busch Wheeler, matriarch of the Anheuser-Busch beer family. She was widely known throughout the horse world simply as Sallie, and was one of the greatest benefactors the horse industry has ever known. She was an imposing woman with a commanding presence and a booming voice. Sallie was a perfect lady in the most gracious, aristocratic sense. When Sallie passed away in 2000, the end was near for "The Garden", and everyone pretty much knew it.

In 1983, I had an opportunity to see a side of Sallie that those who only admired her from a distance would surely miss. I was a member of the judging panel for a week of the winter circuit in Goodyear, Arizona, where Sallie, and her husband Kenny, maintained a winter home in the desert. They had invited a group of us to dinner, and since they were not exhibitors on the circuit, it was fine for us all to accept. Fran was back home taking some clients to a horse show. Just before we left for dinner, I got a phone call that our younger daughter, Julia, then about five years old, had been injured. She was apparently playing in the horse van with a friend, and she fell out the door to the peak. Her young friend approached Fran and said, "Mrs. Dotoli, Julia fell out of the van. But don't worry; she's O.K., because she's not crying". Fran ran to the van to find Julia unconscious. She was rushed to a nearby hospital, and regained consciousness in the ambulance. Fran said Julia was awake and the doctors were running tests on her. I was frantic. Sallie had quietly asked someone in our party what was wrong. Sallie excused herself from the table for a moment, and when she returned, she calmly and without attracting attention walked over and whispered in my ear. "Darlin" she said, with a hint of a southern drawl (Sallie always called people "darlin"), "I heard about that little girl of yours. She's going to be fine, don't you worry. I want you to know that if you need to go home, we'll get you home". Sallie had arranged for a plane home if my family needed me. Julia was fine and I stayed and judged, but that night I became a lifelong fan of Sallie Wheeler.

Many years later, in 2001, I was honored by the United States Equestrian Federation for my service to the horse world. I was awarded the Sallie Busch Wheeler Distinguished Service Award for Contributions to Equestrian Sport. Sallie had recently died, and this new award was being given in tribute to her. The fact that it is given in memory of Sallie made it all the more special. She was a wonderful lady.

*　　*　　*　　*

We had two weeks after Harrisburg to prepare for the Maclay championships at "The Garden". Although we were all disappointed about what happened, none of us felt that it was a failure in our preparation, so we didn't sense any need for drastic measures to be taken. Peter really loved just spending time with the horses. He was meticulous about grooming them, picking out their feet, massaging and wrapping their legs after work, and just doing all the little things that make a horse look and feel its best. We always tried to impress on him the importance of being a good horseman as well as a good rider; and of connecting with the horses. Those two weeks were mostly filled with those types of relaxing activity. Not a lot of high intensity training, just trail rides, hacks, hanging out at the barn, and the occasional light school. By that time of year the horses are tired from the long summer and fall of horse shows every week; any down time that you can give them goes a long way to keep their bodies and minds fresh.

On the Monday before we were to leave for New York, we gave Surf his last light school, and Peter took him out on a trial ride to cool out as he usually did. It was a beautiful sunny day as Surf, and Peter walked through the Norfolk Hunt Club property that abutted ours. As Peter turned Surf toward home, he felt him take a misstep. Surf stumbled and nearly went to his knees; he came up dead lame. Peter jumped off and checked to see if he had picked up a stone in his shoe or there was any other visible injury. He saw nothing. He took the reins over Surf's head and walked him slowly back to the barn. When he got there Peter put Surf in the wash stall, and hurried to get Fran and me.

We had a very lame horse, with three days until we left for the biggest event of the show year - perhaps the biggest event of our careers. Every successful show stable has a support team that is vital to being able to get through a crisis like this: veterinarians, blacksmiths, equine dentists, massage therapists, even acupuncturists. Our first two calls that day were to our blacksmith, Bob McCarthy, and our vet, Dr. Anne Williams. Both had been part of our team for many years, and we trusted them both completely. By the time they got to the barn, Surf could hardly walk out of his stall. After examining Surf, both Bob and Dr. Williams agreed it was a severe stone-bruise. Bob carved the affected area out of the sole of Surf's foot. After he was satisfied that he had gotten all the bruised area, he poulticed both front feet and returned Surf to his stall. Bob, a third-generation blacksmith, who really knows his craft, told us not to worry, that both he and Anne would be back in the morning. Don't worry; right, when everything we worked so hard for is dependent on a wonderful horse that could barely walk. Typically, Peter was far more interested in Surf's being all right than he was about being in the Finals. The last thing on his mind was riding in that class on Sunday. Peter stayed with Surf all day, brushing him, keeping the poultice on, and trying to make him feel better.

The next morning, as planned, Bob and Anne arrived at the barn and removed Surf's poultice. He had improved, but was a long way from being sound. Bob pared away more of the foot, this time removing a section of the hoof wall so that it would not have to bear weight. When Bob left the day before, he went back to his shop and hand-forged a special wide shoe for the affected foot, and made a slightly concaved area at the site of the injury so the metal shoe would not put pressure on the bruise. Bob was a genius when it came to repairing an injured hoof, and everyone knew it, including Dr. Williams, who was there if she was needed, but she knew this was Bob's territory. When Bob finished nailing the shoe on Surf's foot, we took him outside. He walked sound. Peter jogged him down the driveway toward the rest of us, and he stayed sound. Bob assured us that each day it would get even better, and as usual, he was right. By the time we had to ship out for New York, Surf was perfectly sound.

The equitation division in general and the Maclay Finals in particular were in their glory years in the early 1980's. Huge numbers of riders, tremendous quality and depth, large crowds, and flamboyant trainers, all made for lots of excitement. There is no question that being able to show at "The Garden" was a major reason. It was so popular in fact that the finals were under a great deal of stress. So many riders were qualifying, there was not enough time to complete the Maclay in one day. The National's directors made a very controversial decision earlier that year: All the qualifiers would go to Leonia, New Jersey, just across the Hudson River from Manhattan, for an elimination round on Friday, with the best one hundred to move on to New York. Exhibitors were terribly upset. It was the idea of working so hard to qualify, and then never making it to "The Garden" if you made a mistake on Friday. The thought of it was horrible. Parents and grandparents with expensive travel and hotel accommodations would already be in New York City; no trainer wanted to make that call and say, "We're not coming, we didn't make it out of New Jersey". It created a very stressful situation for trainers and riders, and as difficult as it was for us I could just imagine what it was like for exhibitors from California or another distant state.

We left very early Thursday morning for Overpeck Riding Center in Leonia, New Jersey. We never used commercial shipping companies; I shipped all the horses myself. We had a vintage twelve horse van that I had purchased in Florida from a commercial hauler that went out of business, pulled by an equally old single axle cab-over Mack tractor. The rig had a brand new paint job that matched our stable colors, white with forest green trim, and looked great, at least I thought so. I had our girls names inscribed over each headlight; Julia on the left, Annie on the right. We had two students going to Overpeck, and I had both horses in the truck with me. Tracy, our groom, rode with me, with Fran and our two riders leading the way in our car.

Everything that could go wrong to delay our arrival at Overpeck had gone wrong. It was a little after 4 P.M., and we had managed to survive the Cross Bronx Expressway, its countless car skeletons stripped to their chassis as a constant reminder of the penalty of a breakdown. Ahead was the George Washington Bridge to New Jersey, and phase one of the 1982 Maclay Finals. As we crossed the GWB, I found myself on a different wave length from what I usually am in the van. Normally, Tracey and I would be listening to music, joking around and having a good time. Not today, I was uneasy, irritated, put out at having to go to New Jersey at all. After the year Peter had, what did we have to prove at Overpeck? It seemed we had nothing to gain and everything to lose in these preliminaries. Peter had been, we felt, the most consistent equitation rider on the circuit all season. We started late, not going to Florida, but he came out strong in the spring winning the Governors Cup at Saratoga and then ran off an impressive list of major wins through the season. Fran and I felt that consistency was his strongest suit, yet here we were heading into the last of the three finals with no ribbons.

We had begun the finals at the United States Equestrian Team center in Gladstone, New Jersey. It was the first year of the USET Finals, so nobody was quite sure what to expect. Since the class specs called for bigger jumps and the inclusion of a water jump we decided not to take

Surf, fearing we might unravel him before the Medal and Maclay. We leased a horse from a friend, Mitch Steege, that had a lot of experience in the jumper division, and was currently showing in the equitation. Peter was not thrilled at the thought of leaving Surf at home, but understood the reasons why, and approached it with his usual positive attitude. Fran and I thought he rode superbly, but the weekend proved to be our initial setback of the season. Peter wasn't in the ribbons for the first time all year. This was followed closely by our disappointment at Harrisburg.

So there we were, headed for the Maclay Finals with no ribbons, and I was getting very worried about it. I found myself seeking consolation in the fact that Peter had another year of eligibility, but I didn't like thinking that way. Our entire approach to the year had been positive; this was no time to start thinking negatively.

The scene as we arrived at Overpeck didn't help; it was eerie. The winds were swirling, and the jumps in the outdoor schooling rings kept falling down. It was unseasonably warm, and although it wasn't raining, you expected it at any moment. The air pressure kept changing rapidly, causing the big stall tents to lift and then lower; it also made the horses very tense as that kind of pressure variation will do. The horses were nowhere near as tense as the people, however. I had never seen this level of tension at a horse show. Trainers and riders; and especially the top riders were uneasy, and Peter was no exception.

We had two qualifiers with us: Peter and Stacie Fluke, a talented young rider on a new horse named Country Sunshine. They looked like a good match, but Stacie was only thirteen, and her lack of experience was going to be working against her. Everything would have to go perfectly if we were to get both of them through the preliminary round.

That night it poured rain. When we arrived at the stable it was still drizzling, although the major rain had ended. The class was scheduled to begin at 8:00 A.M., but competitors were allowed to school in the indoor arena starting at 6:00 A.M.. Six riders at a time were allowed three minutes of schooling time. Both Peter and Stacie went well, so we ended it there even though you could return for another session if you chose to.

Peter drew 42nd in the order; Stacie 48th. The outdoor schooling ring, was ankle deep in mud. Worse still, the footing was mostly clay, which made it very slippery. We warmed Surf up on the flat and trotted a few cross-rails. When we had Peter canter his first jump, Surf slipped in the mud and crashed through it. They managed to keep "the shiny side up", and Surf wasn't hurt, but he was trembling. When Peter approached the next jump, Surf began backing off and wouldn't go near it. Surf refused to go near the jump two or three times, but since this was not something he had ever done before, we told Peter to just relax and walk for a minute. Meanwhile, Fran and I were dying on the inside. We trotted a few more cross-rails and jumped a couple of bigger jumps, then jogged up to the holding area. We knew we must be very close.

Arriving at the in-gate with a grey horse covered in mud, and the rider in front of you entering the ring, is not the most relaxed way to start the Maclay Finals. While Fran and I revised the plan with Peter, Tracy furiously went to work on Surf's muddy legs and Peter's tack and boots. We were way off our routine. This was not good. There was too much tension. No time for Peter or Surf to relax before they went in to the ring. No time for Peter to collect his thoughts and to focus.

The in-gate person called our number; we were in. The difficult course had taken a heavy toll in major errors. It was challenging for certain, but it also seemed fair. It had no traps or really chancy places, but you had to be very accurate, and because the ring was fairly small, the jumps came up in a hurry. We were confident that, barring a major mistake or a stop, Pete would make the cut, but Surf's crash in the schooling area had us very worried. We had a really scared horse, but we only had to beat 74 of the 174 in the class. After that everyone started fresh again, because these scores did not carry over to the Finals at "The Garden".

"Peter", Fran said, "You can't worry about looking smooth, he is going to be questioning everything out there, he's really scared. You're going to have to just get it done, no matter what it takes, no matter what it looks like, make it happen. Be aggressive, override every jump. Don't take anything for granted. We'll just have to hope that will be good enough". Peter nodded, took a deep breath, and entered the arena. His round was rough and rowdy, lacking any feeling of flow that had always marked his riding; but he had done exactly what we asked, as he always did. Surf was tense and jumping flat so he knocked down the top plank of a three-plank vertical, the sound resonating loudly through the arena

In equitation, a knockdown is only considered a major fault if it is caused by the rider's error. It's the judge's call. The same two judges who were officiating in this round would also judge the finals; A. Thom Brede and Lita Reynolds Wangessteen. The judges had no way of knowing what happened in the schooling ring. They only saw a rough and hectic round. Even if it was good enough to make the cut, would they remember it on Sunday, and subconsciously hold it against Peter? Stacie went soon after

Peter, and under the pressure of the finals for the first time, had made some mistakes. We remained hopeful that both would make the cut.

It was a very long, tense wait until the remaining 126 riders completed the course, and the judges compiled their final list of 100 riders. The list was read in numerical order, and since Peter was number 6, it wasn't long before we could breath a sigh of relief; he had made it. Soon after that, we got that news that Stacie had not. The best that can be said was that everyone was glad it was over. Of the top riders during the year, Lanie Wimberly is the only one I can recall who did not make the cut, but the experience had taken its toll on all of us.

We went back to Overpeck on Saturday morning to school. It was a beautiful day, and almost all the mud was gone. Surf was much more like himself. We all relaxed a little, encouraged by Surf's reaction. The plan for getting everyone to "The Garden" was getting a bit complex. Fran and Peter's parents, Seddon and John, would stay in the city Saturday night and get to sleep early to be ready for the schooling session at 3:30 A..M.. I would leave New Jersey about 1:00 A.M. with Surf and catch a nap in the van. There were no stalls available for equitation horses, so they had to arrive in the city in the middle of the night and stand in the vans.

It was always quite a sight to see all those horse vans lined up on 33rd Street. Even though it was very late, this was New York City, and there was plenty of activity going on. Someone always had to stay with the horses. One year I walked up the ramp to find an old drunk in the truck with the horses. He had lifted Country Sunshine's lip and was offering him a drink from a pint of something in a brown paper bag. "Come on, ol' boy, have a drink with a friend. I love horses", he said. I escorted him back down the ramp and sent him on his way.

Peter had been invited to a party in the city, and was disappointed that we asked him not to go. He went to bed right after dinner. The partying would have to wait.

On Sunday, the day of the Finals, a schooling hunter class began at 6:00 A.M.. It was a very short course that allowed everyone a chance to get a round under his or her belt before it really counted. The class was judged as a hunter class on the jumping style of the horse, and by two different judges from those responsible for the Finals. The class went really well. Surf was relaxed, he jumped softly and easily. You could always tell when Surf was tense, his back would get very stiff, and he would hit the jumps. We called it the "braille system". Not this day, however - he was at his best on this day and was pinned third behind two super horses. Sandy

Nielsen, Peter's friend, remarked that it was good luck, because she had been third in the special hunter class at Harrisburg and won the Medal. We were thrilled. Now, if we could only build on that in the Finals, it could be a great day.

When the Maclay course was finally built, Peter and Fran and I walked it with the other 99 riders and their trainers. Again, it seemed quite difficult, but nothing that couldn't be ridden well if you were strong and accurate. Much of it seemed built perfectly for us; more left leads than right, long lines followed by very short ones. No pair backed up after a long line better than Peter and Surf. There were also some interesting options where Christine Jones Tauber, the course designer, wanted you to make decisions. We were a little worried about a narrow jump on the short end of the ring, which was partially hidden by another jump. Surf sometimes didn't react well if he was surprised by a jump.

Peter went 69th, so we sat together and watched the first twenty or so rounds. The course took its toll as many of the top riders had problems. Michaela Murphy had a mistake at the first fence. Clea Newman made an error. Medal winner Sandy Nielsen struggled and lost a stirrup. Californian Linda Medvene had an excellent round. Louis Jacobs had a nice trip. Alan Karotkin had trouble with a very quiet in-and-out. Our plan seemed to hold up to the early rides, so we decided to stick to it.

Once again, Surf schooled superbly, and Fran and I began to get a very good feeling about the day. We took our time in the warm up ring so as not to send any messages of tenseness or hurriedness to Surf. Finally it was time. We went over our plan; Peter was focused but calm. The moment seemed strangely without pressure, entirely different from Overpeck.

When Peter and Surf entered the ring, the crowd grew very quiet as it does whenever one of those ten or twelve special riders get ready to begin their trips. The round began with that beautiful forward rhythm that had become Peter and Surf's trademark. There it was; it was back; that indelible picture of the big grey horse and this handsome, blond young man who always made it so obvious how much they loved what they do. The oxer to the end jump rode like magic. The long-to-short distances, as expected, were breathtaking. Two-thirds of the way around, they have been close to perfect. Looming at the end of the course was the last jump, another combination. We knew the error at Harrisburg would not be repeated. Peter learns his lesson well. If I had to bet the farm on one thing, it would be that there would not be an extra stride in that combination at the end of the course. As they cleared the last jump, the crowd erupted. I have never witnessed crowd support like it. In addition to being respected as a rider, Peter was extremely popular with his peers as well as all the trainers. They all knew how hard he worked. Years later, Jenny Iverson (Shwartz), one of the other top riders of that time, told me; "We all knew down deep we couldn't beat him, because he would always outwork us".

Fran and I ran to the out gate to meet them, dodging our way through all the people in the walkway. Peter jumped off and gave Surf two big pats, then loosened his girth. He turned and gave Fran and Tracy each a big hug. Not much needed to be said, we all knew. Tracy took Surf, and we went to watch the rest of the first round. After 75 riders had competed; the next standby list was read. Peter's number was the last one to be announced - we were on top. Fran and I were thrilled but not surprised, Peter and Surf had been wonderful. After all 100 had completed their rounds, the final list didn't change at the top. Peter was still in first place. Linda Medvene from Santa Barbara, California, and trained by Paul Valliere, was second.

Thirty would return for the flat phase of the Maclay Finals. The riders and horses are all brought into the ring as a group, and the judges work them at the posting and sitting trot and at the canter. They often ask other tests as well, such as the counter-canter or riding without stirrups. The riders are expected to affect their horses in the correct manner and to do it while exhibiting classic riding style.

The chosen thirty all gathered in the underbelly of Madison Square Garden. As always, a makeshift schooling area about the size of a single tennis court was constructed at the top of the ramp leading to 33rd Street. It was really just a few inches of dirt laid down on the cement floor. Its small size alone made it almost unusable, but in addition to its tiny size, there were two mammoth concrete pillars in the middle of it. To call it a schooling area was really stretching it, but to anyone in the horse world, it was the greatest place in the world. At any other show you would complain about the conditions, but not at The Garden, during the first week in November, if you were fortunate enough to be there, nothing was a problem.

As we waited for word from the judges to enter the ring, everyone lined up roughly in the order of the call-back. When the signal came down, Linda trotted off past us. Her horse lightly bumped Surf as she went past, and he pinned his ears and raised his head. She entered the ring first, with the elegance that made her so tough to beat on the flat. The mind games were in full force. We should have had Peter ready for that; but we didn't. I could see that he was agitated, but I couldn't imagine him coming unglued over it.

We expected the flat work to be difficult for us. Surf doesn't like to be crowded, and thirty horses on the Garden floor is really tight. The other trainers and riders seemed worried about getting too close to the rail because of the crowd. That left about a three foot lane next to the wall. The Garden floor is sunken, which put spectators almost at eye level to the horses. Surf was never bothered by people and noise, so we planned to use that lane to help keep him by himself. That strategy put Peter a little out of view, but since he was on top, we knew the judges would find him.

The flat work was very long compared to other years; both directions, all gaits, with and without stirrups. Surf had grown somewhat tense during this phase, and Peter had his hands full when the horses lined up at the end, but he handled it well. The new list cut the final group to twenty, and we had dropped to second behind Linda.

Peter was frustrated by being dropped, but Fran and I were glad. Holding the top spot from start to finish is a difficult task, and there was still a long way to go before the 1982 Maclay Champion was pinned. Knowing Peter, being second would only intensify his effort in the next round over jumps. After we discussed it, Peter agreed and seemed more at ease. If Linda had still been second at this point, she would have had the advantage of having everything to gain and nothing to lose. We preferred to have Peter lay down one of his second-round gems as he had done all year, and let the pressure be on Linda to match it. Of course, there would be eighteen other excellent young riders all trying to add to the pressure for the top few. Karen McKelvey, Louis Jacobs, and Lori Hall were all close, and each of them was capable of sprinting past us if we faltered.

The next couple of hours had to be the longest of our lives. The Garden was cleared, which signaled the end of the morning session. In the afternoon, the second half of the Maclay Championship would follow an international jumping competition and a saddle horse class. Fran and I took our group of about twelve people and went to a little cafeteria that we hoped would be away from the horse show crowd. Fortunately it was. We had a very relaxing lunch and a lot of laughs. When we got back to the Garden, the pressure began to rapidly build again. A number of well meaning friends and supporters came down to the schooling ring and said things like; "We're all counting on you, Pete", and "Too bad you got moved down to second". We asked two of our former riders to take Peter to the top balcony away from everyone, and to stay with him while Fran and I handled the well wishers.

As always, the second round started with the twentieth-place rider going first, so we got a chance to watch a few rounds before we had to school. It was another well thought-out course, and if the first one favored our strengths, this one could have been built by us, it was so perfect. Schooling went well, except that the course contained a trot jump to a no-stride bounce that we wanted to school over, and it became a little tense trying to find a time that we could use all the standards that we needed. Finally, we were down to the last few to school and Paul Valliere wanted the bounce also, so we all set one up. It was no problem, and although Peter had been worried about it, he seemed fine now.

Finally, we were on deck. Peter walked Surf to the rear of the schooling area to get mentally prepared, then back to the in-gate. He urged Surf forward, as close to the gate as possible to allow Surf's eyes time to adjust to the bright lights of the arena. The gates opened and Victor Hugo-Vidal began to announce who was next. At that moment something happened that I had never witnessed before. When the people in the stands saw them, the usually conservative and proper horse show crowd began to scream and clap until the noise level was so high, you could barely hear Victor on the PA any longer. They were making it very clear who their favorites were. We knew this would not unsettle Peter, but would instead help him. He thrives on riding under pressure and would welcome the crowd's support.

Peter went to the center of the ring, and the arena went to absolute pin-drop silence. When he caught his canter, his pace and tempo were perfect - vintage Peter and Surf. When they jumped the first fence, Fran and I looked at each other. We had been watching Peter ride for five years, and the rhythm that he begins with is crucial to his results. We both knew this was going to be special. Peter and Surf owned the course. The long lines weren't long, and the short lines weren't short. Their transition to the trot and the trot bounce, were flawless. The round was even and flowing. It was exciting, it had charisma. This was the best Peter had ever been - he had saved this awesome effort for his moment on the biggest stage. When they jumped the final fence, I thought the roof would come off Madison Square Garden. The noise was deafening. I clapped, but I couldn't whistle. It is impossible to whistle if you can't stop smiling.

We were as sure as you can be at a subjectively judged event that no rider who went before us had been good enough to beat us. The only rider who went into this round ahead of us, Linda Medvene, was now in the ring. Tracy held Surf, while Peter ran up the stairs with Fran and me to watch. Linda began matching him jump for jump. She was outstanding. Then, suddenly, a mistake: Linda's horse left the ground early and she got behind in the air a little. She recovered well, but ran into more trouble when her horse lost his lead for a couple of strides on a turn. The errors would cost her. We thought she would probably get moved down, but how far.

We all waited in the schooling area for additional testing to be announced. The Maclay always has one final test of the top four or sometimes six (the number to be tested, and the test itself, are at the discretion of the judges). We tried to anticipate who would make the additional testing. Jill Sternberg was exceptional, but had started quite a way back in the round of twenty. Bryce Cabot from Canada was also impressive. A number of riders had been good, including Linda, but we felt confident that we must be leading.

The wait was longer than usual, until finally we heard why. The judges had decided that there was no need for additional testing. It was the first time this had ever happened in the long and glorious history of the Maclay Championship. Victor announced the ten numbers to come back into the ring for ribbons, but it was in numerical order, not in order of standing. Trainers and riders were coming over to us in droves to congratulate us. We were grateful but uneasy. The results were still not official, nothing had been announced. We had seen strange things happen over the years. Maybe the two most important people, the judges, had seen the results differently. We saw it all unfold from the end of the ring, the judges watch from the side; what if it looked different to them? Maybe we were in for a huge letdown.

As is the custom at all the finals, they announced the ribbons in reverse order; from tenth place forward. "In tenth place, from Wilton, Connecticut, and trained by Mr. Ronnie Mutch and Mr. Tim Kees, is Mr. Peter Lombardo". As Victor worked his way toward the winner, Fran and I just stood there frozen, afraid to say or do anything for fear we would jinx it. "In fourth place" Victor's wonderful deep baritone voice continued, "From Santa Barbara, California, Miss Linda Medvene". "Linda is trained by Mr. Paul Valliere". That drop into fourth was huge, her mistakes had cost her. The unimaginable now seemed possible. "Taking the yellow ribbon all the way home to British Columbia, Canada is Mr. Bryce Cabot". "Mr. Cabot is trained by Hunterdon Incorporated". Only two left, I could feel my heart beating. "The reserve champion for the 1982 Maclay finals is" Victor paused for what seemed like an hour, "Miss Jill Sternberg from Colts Neck, New Jersey". We did it, I grabbed Fran and hugged her. "Jill is trained by her mother Mrs. Sandy Sternberg". "And now" Victor paused again, "The 1982 Maclay champion from Medfield, Massachusetts, Mr. Peter Wylde. Peter is trained by a husband and wife team, Mrs. Fran and Mr. Joe Dotoli". Peter gave Surf a pat on the neck and asked him to step forward. He burst into a big smile and removed his hat to accept his ribbon revealing his long blond hair. The crowd at the Garden was still standing and cheering. The attendants rolled out the red carpet from the side entrance of the ring to the presentation area. Fran and I were escorted out by the ring master and were presented with the Woodrow G. Gatehouse Memorial Trophy as the winning trainers of the Maclay Champion.

Peter and "Native Surf", 1982 Maclay Champions.
Photo courtesy of Freudy Photos.

For me personally, one of the most gratifying moments occurred during the presentation of the Gatehouse Trophy. I looked over at the trainer's corner, and could see that it was in a greater uproar than the rest of the Garden. The people who wanted to win every bit as much as we did were happy for us. Timmy Kees was jumping up and down, Paul Valliere was waving his arms. They were all there, all the people whom we admired as trainers were happy about who won. They competed to the last stride, but when it was over, they knew we had a clean win, and they were happy for us. The legendary Ronnie Mutch later called it, "the least controversial win in the history of the Maclay".

Back in the stands, George Morris congratulated us on doing a "fine job" with Peter. He called him a "real class act". He said he looked like "another Homfeld", and then he repeated, "another Homfeld". I thought about Harrisburg and Frances Rowe's quote, and the way Peter handled his setback that day. "Homfeld", I thought, "nice company".

Fran, Peter, his parents, and I were whisked upstairs to the press conference. The interview was held in a very fancy room somewhere in the building. The room was filled with people. Waiters in tuxedos were serving champagne. Peter was on the phone with his brother, MacRae, who was not able to be there. He was the first person Peter wanted to call. "MacRae, I won, can you believe it, I won". There were television crews, and lots of journalists, and not just horse magazines, real newspapers. *The Boston Globe* was there, and the *New York Times* - *The Times* for God sake. The reporter from *The Times* asked Fran "what are you most proud of here today"? Fran shot back, "I'm most proud of the fact that a real horseman won here today". It was the perfect answer.

That night Peter finally got to go out and party, while I had to face the reality that we had a tired horse that had to get back to Massachusetts. Fran would stay in New York, and Tracy and I would take Surf home. It was a long four-hour drive after all we had been through, but that is the reality of a life with horses. Actually, the only unusual thing was that Fran and Peter weren't there with us.

We finally got off the highway in Milford, Massachusetts, onto Route 109. Our farm was just off 109 about twenty miles ahead. It was late, and I was tired, and I was running the van pretty hard. I'm sure I was well above the speed limit. We crossed the line into Medway, then through Millis. We rolled down the long hill approaching the Medfield line. Only a few more minutes, and we would be home. The van roared across the town line into Medfield. Suddenly, on both sides of the road, we saw flashing blue lights, and lots of them. "Oh no, don't tell me the day is going to end like this", I said, half to Tracy, and half to no one in particular. Then something really cool happened. One police cruiser pulled in front of us, and one behind us. They were giving us a police escort from the town line to the stable. With sirens blaring and lights flashing, the town of Medfield was welcoming home their heroes.

There is something special about small towns. That spring, Peter would ride on a float in the Memorial Day parade. That is what winning at The Garden meant to non-horse-people. They might not understand horses, but they understood what it meant in any sport to win at Madison Square Garden.

The Wolf

When Peter was sixteen, we all felt it was time to get his jumper career started. In today's horse show world there are numerous low level jumper divisions; children's, training, schooling, and many level 1 and 2 divisions to begin riding jumpers. Junior riders in the early 1980's, learned to ride in the hunter and equitation divisions and didn't move on to a jumper unless and until they were very accomplished. There were no low classes; everything was big, really big. Up to this time Peter had competed only in those two divisions, and rode anything in the barn that needed to be ridden or shown. We shopped around for a horse that could give him some experience in the jumper division, an older horse or one with manageable soundness problems.

Peter could not control his enthusiasm. He began reading all the classified ads in every periodical he could find (Fortunately, there was no internet at this time). Most often, good show horses are found through trainers networking with each other, not in classified ads, but reading all the ads kept him busy and gave him less time to nag us about what horses we had found. After a few weeks of this I agreed to call about one of the ads he picked out, only so that he would calm down. The ad simply read:

15.1 h. bay g. Q.H.
Jumper experience
$10,000 o.b.o.

15.1 h. refers to the size of the horse. A horse is measured from the ground to the top of the withers, the highest point on a horse's back, just before the neck. The unit of measurement is the hand (abbreviated as "h"). A hand is four inches, and the term comes from the days when horses were measured by starting at ground level and putting one hand over the other up the front leg, until you reached the withers. 15.1 hands is quite small for a jumper. The g. means the horse is a gelding, or a castrated male. Q.H. stands for Quarter Horse, an American breed used mostly for Western riding. As in most ads, the o.b.o. means "or best offer". The ad ended with a Connecticut telephone number.

I called and spoke to a young man who sounded like a very motivated seller; he didn't have time to ride him, he was going to Florida for the winter and couldn't afford to bring the horse, he really needed to sell him, etc. etc. During the conversation, I realized that I knew the horse. David Hopper, a well known New York horseman, brought him out as a young horse in the preliminary jumper division. The horse was definitely not without talent. I called David, who confirmed my memory and agreed that the horse had talent. However, he also recalled that the horse was difficult to deal with.

Peter and I, along with Peter's dad, drove to Connecticut late the next afternoon. It was dark by the time we got there. The young man that I spoke to on the phone met us at the local stable where he boarded the horse. The stable had a small indoor arena so we were able to try the horse after dark. It did not take long to figure out why the owner was so anxious to sell; he was terrified of the horse. When we asked him to ride the horse first, so we could watch, his face became ashen. Slowly, he got the horse from its stall, tacked him up, and climbed aboard. The horse was smaller than I remembered, much smaller. The 15.1 hands in the ad may even have been an exaggeration, he looked like he barely made 15 hands. He was seal brown and built like the Quarter Horse that he was, with very muscular, large hind quarters and a topline which sloped a little down-hill from back to front. His small feet made me wonder about his long term soundness.

After watching the owner walk around for almost fifteen minutes, apparently unable or unwilling to do much more, I decided to just put Peter on, and see what we could do with him. Peter figured the horse out almost immediately. Despite his size, this horse was game. He was a bit unorthodox, but he definitely wanted to jump clean. We didn't know how fit he was, so we didn't want to do too much and hurt him. We finished up by jumping a couple of very big jumps. The next day we made the man an offer, and he jumped at it. I really felt we may have found a "diamond in the rough". Certainly for what we paid for him, we couldn't go wrong. We named him "The Wolf" as in "Peter and the Wolf".

We quickly found out why that young man was so afraid of The Wolf. He was as ornery a horse as I had ever dealt with. He would snarl at you in his stall, and he meant it. He would kick out if you tried to brush him or if you attempted to tighten his girth; and he aimed for you. On the van, he would challenge every other horse on the truck. He definitely had the equine version of a Napoleonic complex.

The Wolf approached his job with the same feisty attitude. He almost defied the jumps to remain in this path. He would attack the jump, ears flat back, and then explode off the ground. Peter's relaxed riding style fit him perfectly. Peter had no fear of The Wolf or any other horse. On The Wolf, he didn't have to be restrained by the precision and rigidity of the equitation and hunter divisions. "Peter and The Wolf" seemed to fly to victory after victory. With Peter's care, The Wolf's personality visibly changed, but he never became a pet. He was never one you could trust if you weren't there to oversee him.

After discussing the idea with the Wyldes, we decided it would be beneficial for Peter to have input from someone who was competitive at the Grand Prix level. Peter suggested Norman Dello Joio, and Norman agreed to help coach Peter in the jumper divisions. The following season, they were champions in the junior jumper division at the Washington International Horse Show and the International Jumping Derby in Portsmouth Rhode Island, and they represented New England on a Zone 1 team that won a bronze medal in the Prix de States at the Pennsylvania National Horse Show. The Wolf was a wonderful horse, and after a while his aggressiveness became more his trade mark and somehow became less threatening. He was a real competitor, and you had to love him for it.

Peter and "The Wolf" jumping the water at the International Jumping Derby, Portsmouth, Rhode Island, 1982. Peter is wearing the leading rider sash. Dr. Robert "Doc" Rost is judging. Photo courtesy of Judith Buck Photos.

The 1983 Medal Finals
Harrisburg, Pennsylvania

The indoor fall circuit always marks the end of another show season. As the summer came to an end, and indoor shows drew closer, no junior rider had been more dominant than Peter. He had been consistent in the equitation division with Surf, and ridden numerous hunters successfully, both from within our barn as well as "catch rides" from other trainers. His jumper career had really accelerated with the purchase of "The Wolf". The little Quarter Horse who seemed to defy the jumps to get out of his way had been winning classes at all the major shows.

As always, the Pennsylvania National is the first of the indoor shows and hosts what was then the American Horse Shows Association Medal Finals (in recent years the AHSA has become the USEF – United States Equestrian Federation). This was Peter's last year of eligibility as a junior rider, and after having won the Maclay the previous year, he was a favorite to win the Medal, the class that his friend Sandy Nielsen had won the year before.

In addition to the Medal Finals, the Penn National is also the venue for the end-of year junior jumper championships, the Prix de States. Riders and their horses ride as a team that represents a region of the country. The United States usually fields ten teams, and riders qualify by doing well during the year. Canada and Mexico often compete in the event as well. It is a young rider's first step toward international competition. It's a wonderful event, but it also puts added pressure on riders doing both the Prix de States and the Medal. The team competition for the Prix de States on Saturday night often lasted until after midnight. The Medal began with a 6:00 A.M. course walk on Sunday morning.

Any junior who qualified for both, wanted to ride in both, and Peter was no exception. He had qualified to represent U.S. Zone 1, which includes the six New England states, with The Wolf; and then would ride in the Medal the next morning on Surf. Norman Dello Joio was not able to come for the class, so we schooled Peter. This was not unusual, as very often we did train Peter in the jumpers as well as the other divisions. Norman's role was as much a consultant as anything.

It was an exciting evening. In the team competition, Peter and the Wolf had a respectable four-fault score to help their team win the bronze medal. The final results were in doubt until the last horse. We left the arena at almost midnight with the adrenaline still flowing. The four of us - Fran, Peter, Tracy and I - headed to the stable area to take care of The Wolf. Actually, it would be more accurate to say we went to watch Peter take care of The Wolf.

Peter had a very specific routine with each of the horses that he rode, regardless of whether or not he owned them, and he was adamant about doing each phase correctly. First was unraveling the perfectly tied braids that he had constructed just a few hours before. He stood on a three-step ladder, carefully cutting the yarn that holds the braid together and being equally careful not to cut any of the hairs that make up the mane. A full bath was next, and his horses always stood contentedly as the warn water cascaded over their tired bodies. A curved piece of aluminum called a scrapper removes the majority of the excess water. Back at the stall, Peter towel dried each leg as prevention against a very common and serious conditional called scratches. All four legs were massaged with liniment, then perfectly wrapped with rest bandages. Then, Peter applied Vaseline to the horse's heels. Next, the mane and tail were picked out, a bag of carrots offered as a reward, and off to the stall. When that was all completed, Peter would remove any manure from the stall before we could leave. This is a routine that he still performs today with each of his Grand Prix horses, including braiding each horse himself. These quiet times have always been his opportunity to connect with his horses, and he still treasures them.

This night, or I should say morning, Peter emerged from the wash stall with The Wolf. He walked back toward the stall area to continue the routine. The rhythmical "clip clop" of The Wolf's steel shoes on the concrete floor closely followed Peter. Tracy took the lead shank from Peter, who knelt down to start drying Wolf's legs. The Prix de States had been over for an hour.

"Peter" I said, "it's 12:45, the hotel is forty minutes from here, and we have a big day tomorrow. Why don't you let Tracy finish up, so you can get some sleep"? He looked at me as if I had just slapped him, then what he said made me feel like I was the one who was slapped, "We've come too far doing it like this; please don't make me stop now". He was right. Peter finished his routine with The Wolf about 1:30, when we arrived back at the hotel it was after 2:00 A.M. Three and a half hours later we were back at the barn, ready to walk the Medal course.

*   *   *   *

Most of the trainers were not very happy with the course. It was nothing specific, no particularly scary jump or a treacherous line. The problem was more that the course seemed to have no flow to it. It was just a jumble of jumps and lines. Designing a course for a national championship is very complicated. The course must be difficult enough to separate almost 300 of the best young riders in the country, but not so tough as to be dangerous. It is easy as a course designer to think you have it, only to find out when the class starts that you have missed. But by then, it is too late to make any changes.

Peter's round was certainly not his best ever, but we were confident that he would return near the top of the class. When the final standby list was read, we were extremely disappointed to hear that he had been called back thirtieth out of thirty-five to return. The arena was buzzing about it. Some trainers, naturally, were secretly happy. With Peter out of the way, it was anyone's class to win.

With such a low placing, Peter could have folded his tent. Certainly, he had to be physically and mentally exhausted. He could have just gone into the second round, gone through the motions, and gone home. But that would not be Peter Wylde. Instead he attacked. He rode the second round with nothing to lose. We planned all the most difficult options that the course offered. After all thirty-five had ridden, Peter moved all the way from thirtieth to eighth.

One of the judges was Victor Hugo-Vidal, the same man who had announced at The Garden the previous year. Victor was famous for testing riders more than anyone else when he judged. If he kept testing, and we kept moving up, maybe - just maybe - we still had a chance. The judges brought the top eight back into the ring. When they were all lined up in the center, each was asked to change horses with one of the others. Changing horses is the ultimate test in an equitation class. For most young riders it is very difficult, but Peter always rode so many different horses every day, that we considered it a huge advantage. In addition, Surf was really hard to ride if you weren't used to him which also became a positive for us. After they tested, Peter moved up to fifth. "Please" I whispered to no one in particular, "please, just one more test". "Come on Victor; don't stop now, just one more". But not today, the class was over, and Peter finished fifth.

Perhaps Peter wasn't as sharp as he could have been. Perhaps he was just too mentally and physically drained to make it happen, but both his horses were properly cared for, and that was more important to him than any ribbon could possibly be. I was never more proud of him.

"Native Surf" retirement ceremony at The New England Equitation Championships, pictured with some of his former riders. Left to right: Allen Keeley (ringmaster), Fran, "Surf", Peter, Annie Dotoli, Julia Dotoli, Leila Wood, D.M.V., Wendy Barquin. Photo courtesy of Catherin Cammett Photography.

The Post Junior Years

After completing his junior career and graduating from Noble and Greenough School, Peter took a year off from school to ride, before beginning his freshman year at Tufts University, just outside of Boston, in Medford, Massachusetts. He made the decision to really enjoy his college experience and not try to keep showing, with the exception of the summer months, during his four years at Tufts. For the most part, Peter kept to that plan. He did, however, join the Tufts University equestrian team. The IHSA (Intercollegiate Horse Shows Association) is a very different experience from showing on the circuit. Riders on each team show up at the host college's stable or a nearby stable associated with the college and draw for horses that are provided by that school. Peter loved being a part of it, and thoroughly enjoyed working with the other team members and sharing his now-substantial background with them. The most prestigious honor that can be achieved in the IHSA is to win the Cacchione Cup at the national finals which are held at the end of the school year. Peter won the Cacchione Cup while a member of the Tufts team.

After graduating from Tufts in 1998, Peter opened his own stable. He called his new venture Bondurant Inc. Like most young trainers, he spent a great deal of his time trying to become established. His first Grand Prix horse was a mare named Tootsie. Although she was not a world-class mare, she always tried hard and won ten grand prix ribbons. His first really special horse was another mare; Can Can. She was only 15.3 hands, but she had talent, was brave, and no horse tried harder. After a number of good finishes with Can Can, Peter had a real breakthrough when he was named leading rider at the prestigious Washington International Horse Show in 1993.

The progress that Peter made in building his business and his reputation would have been enough to satisfy most young professional riders, but not Peter. He came to the conclusion that the only way to become an elite rider was to compete against the best in the world. So, after spending a great deal of time and effort developing Bondurant, he closed its doors in 1994 and moved to Europe. It took a lot of courage to leave everything behind that was going so well, but he wanted to test himself against the best every day, and that meant leaving home for the other side of the Atlantic. Fortunately, Peter's being able to take Can Can with him gave him a huge head start towards proving himself to the Europeans. Can Can and Peter competed in 17 European Grand Prix and had a ribbon in almost every one.

After two years, Peter returned to the U.S. to ride for Dan Lufkin at Chestnut Ridge Farm in Millbrook, N.Y. His riding career was about to take another quantum leap. He continued to compete on Can Can, winning the President's Cup at the 1996 Washington International. While at Chestnut Ridge, Peter was fortunate to get the ride on two new horses: Macanudo Very Well St. George and Macanudo DeNiro (Macanudo cigars were Peter's main sponsor at that time). All three were world-class horses.

During this period Peter split his time between showing in Europe and the U.S. and was having a good deal of success in both places. Then, in 1999, Peter got the opportunity that he always wanted and that had managed to elude him. He was selected to represent the United States at the Pan-American Games in Winnipeg, Canada. Finally, he would get to wear the "pink coat" of the United States Equestrian Team. And he did not disappoint the selectors. He rode Macanudo DeNiro to the Team and Individual Silver Medals. Fran and I felt badly that neither of us was able to go to Winnipeg to support him, but it just wasn't possible that year. Because of his successes, Peter was named Equestrian of the Year by *The Chronicle of the Horse* for the first time.

Peter at the Pan American Games, 1999.
Photo courtesy of James Leslie Parker Photography

The next year, after weighing all the possibilities and making some very difficult decisions for the direction of his career, Peter moved back to Europe permanently. If you have never been to Europe, it might be hard for an American horse person to understand why a top Grand Prix rider would want to leave his home, family, friends, and all he had worked for and head to Europe. Actually, there are a number of reasons. In the U.S. we are inundated with sports. We have what we consider the four major sports; football, basketball, baseball, and hockey. Then we have intercollegiate versions of all four, plus soccer, figure skating, gymnastics, track and field, and many others. Somewhere buried in that never- ending array is equestrian sport.

In Europe there is soccer (they call it "football"), and horse sport, and not much else. Riders compete in front of huge audiences and packed houses. They are like rock stars. You can go to a show and watch in person, then go home and watch the same show on television that night. Since many of the countries are small and travel less of an issue, riders from all over the continent compete. National pride is a big part of the excitement of the shows. Then there is the financial appeal. Because the big shows have sold-out performances and television rights, they want the best horses and riders at their show. The monetary incentives for the "A" list of riders can be quite substantial. Finally, there is the level of competition, which doesn't get any better. While in recent years the Americans have closed the gap, especially with two consecutive Olympic Team Gold Medals, the epicenter of show jumping is in Europe.

The 2001 World Cup
Gothenburg, Sweden

As soon as we got word that Peter had qualified for the 2001 World Cup finals in Gothenburg Sweden, Fran and I began making plans to be there. It was his first World Cup, and since we had missed the Winnipeg Pan Am Games, we definitely wanted to be with him in Sweden. We bought our plane tickets and made a reservation at the same hotel where Peter and many other riders were staying. Everything was all set and ready to go. Then, a few weeks before the start, bad things began to happen. News was coming from Europe of an outbreak of Hoof and Mouth Disease, which is extremely contagious and very serious. It affects all species of hoofed animas, not just horses. About two weeks before the scheduled start of the World Cup, Holland closed its borders. No animals could go in or out, and Peter and his horses were in Holland. Sweden added to the confusion by issuing a statement that all horses competing in the World Cup had to be in the country 14 days before the start. We didn't know whether to cancel our flights and hotel while we still could or to take a chance. We decided to go for it and hope it all worked out.

A Swedish court case finally allowed the seven horses and three riders stuck in Holland to travel. They could go to Denmark for five days, and if there were no outbreaks, they could continue on to Gothenburg. The horses finally arrived in Sweden on Wednesday, the day before the first round of the World Cup. That was the same day we arrived.

Fran and I were managing Ox Ridge Hunt Club in Darien, Connecticut at this time. When we left Darien for Gothenburg, there were signs of spring everywhere. Flowers were beginning to bloom, and the sun felt warm. A far different climate greeted us when we landed in Sweden. It was still very much winter in Gothenburg. The sky was battleship grey, and the cold was bone-chilling. To add to the grim feeling, all the buildings were constructed out of stone, grey stone.

I felt much better once we found our way to the beautiful sports complex where the World Cup was being held. It was a very attractive 20,000 seat arena. Even more impressive was how the walls, the VIP area, the ring and especially the jumps, were decorated. Adjacent to the arena was a very spacious vendor area. I'm not sure exactly how big it was, but you could have used acres as a unit of measurement. It was jammed with all sorts of horse equipment, clothing, jewelry, books and other horse-related things for sale.

A World Cup held in Gothenburg, is not a "stand alone" event. It is part of a very popular horse show. It is just the one coliseum ring, and it is usually busy well into the night. Because of that format, Peter had three horses with him. His World Cup horse was Macanuto DeNiro, with whom he had been so successful at the Pan Am Games. The second horse was a chestnut gelding named Job, a really good speed horse. The third horse was a mare that he had been recently sent to sell. Her name was Fein Cera. She was tall, elegant, and very well bred.

The first class was a speed class. Peter rode Job and won by a huge margin, nearly two seconds. In international competition, that is almost unheard of. While the class was exciting, the pinning was almost more so. At the big European shows, the ribbons are actually put on the horse down under the stands out of sight. After a short pause, the lights dimmed almost to complete darkness, a spot-light lit the in-gate and tunnel leading down to the schooling area under the stands. Suddenly, blasting over the speaker system, Bruce Springsteen's "Born in the USA". Galloping out of the tunnel, full tilt, helmet in hand and blond hair and ribbon flying came Peter. The crowd was clapping its hands in rhythm to the music as they roared approval and Peter and Job galloped all the way around the arena. "What a great start" I thought.

The next morning, Fran, Peter and I caught a ride to the arena on the shuttle. Like many of the big shows in Europe, another perk for the riders was a free shuttle back and forth to the venue. Its use is restricted to the riders and their guests. Rodrigo Pessoa from Brazil was already in the vehicle when we jumped in to get out of the cold. As the car pulled away from the curb, Peter leaned over and said "Rodrigo, this is Fran and Joe Dotoli, these are the people who taught me how to ride". Fran and I leaned across to shake the hand of one of the world's greatest riders. "Now

Peter", I said smiling, "You know the only thing we ever claimed was that we didn't screw you up". Peter chuckled and continued, "Not riding- wise maybe, but what about all those years of therapy"? He thought he was so funny. Actually, although I'm not sure Rodrigo knew what to make of us, it was funny. Just as important, the points were made: Peter gave us credit for teaching him how to ride, and we freely admitted the success was because of him. Peter never forgot the people who helped him along the way, from Patty Perry, the first person to teach him, to Conrad Homfeld who coaches him at some of the biggest international events, Peter has always had a long memory.

The World Cup's opening round is a speed course. It is vital to do well in this phase because it often ends up being the separating factor among the top riders at the end of the three days of competition. A speed class in a relatively small indoor coliseum is not DeNiro's strong suit. He is a massive horse that is very careful and more than a little spooky. He jumps really clean because of that, but it usually takes a while to develop. He is at his best on the big outdoor, galloping courses. Peter got De Niro around with no faults, but it took everything he had. It certainly didn't help that DeNiro had not competed in five weeks because of the Hoof and Mouth scare. They finished quite low in the standings, but we all knew there was a long way to go.

In Saturday's second phase, Peter managed to get a really nervous DeNiro through the first round, but couldn't hold it together in the jump-off, and they had quite a few faults. Then Peter would make a decision that would change the course of his career, and in a way, show jumping history.

Peter was understandably a bit down about his World Cup to this point. Job was going great, winning two classes, but it was the World Cup that brought us all to Sweden. Between classes, Peter would come to the stands and sit with our group; his mom and dad, Hank Nooren (one of the great names in European show jumping, who was a big help to Peter during his time there), Conrad Homfeld, Fran and myself. We formed a little cocoon around him so he could focus. At a European event like the World Cup, there is a constant stream of autograph-seekers and well-wishers, and Peter needed to concentrate. At one point he leaned over to me and said, "I'm thinking of changing horses, what do you think"? I tried to hide the fact that I had no idea that was even allowed. "Who would you switch to"? I asked. "The other horse I brought, Fein Cera, I've only ridden her a couple of times, but she is incredibly scopy."

I'm not sure I ever really gave him an answer, I was pretty confused as to how that would work. I don't think it mattered, Peter had pretty much made up his mind. The change was made to Fein Cera for the final day of the Cup.

The third and final day of the World Cup is two rounds over a gigantic course. The class almost always shakes things up because so few horses can jump a course that big, never mind jump it twice in the span of a couple of hours. Fein Cera got stronger as she went, giving some indication of what the future held. She had four faults in the first round, and no faults in the second, only one of two horses to go clean in that second round. Peter jumped all the way up to a sixth-place finish. He was thrilled, especially with the effort Fein Cera made without the benefit of the earlier, easier courses that all the other horses got to jump during the week. It turned out to be a great World Cup after all.

There was one problem with Fein Cera's showing that day, however. She was, after all, for sale and had just become a very saleable item. Peter didn't have much time to enjoy his World Cup success if he was to keep the ride on her. Through a lot of hard work and the cooperation of her owners, a group was put together to buy Fein Cera. Peter got to keep riding his new superstar.

2002
World Equestiran Games
Jerez, Spain

The Olympic Games, as in many sports, are the most important event in show jumping. However, while they don't get the media attention of the Olympics, the World Equestrian Games hold an equally elevated place of importance among those involved in the sport. The World Games, or WEG as they are known, are also held every four years, but scheduled so that they alternate every two years with the Olympics. The disciplines that are included are show jumping, eventing, dressage, reining, vaulting, endurance and driving.

While there is a team element to show jumping at WEG, unlike the Olympics, it is individual accomplishment that is featured. The format is very different from any other equestrian event. The horse/rider combinations must jump four rounds of international caliber courses over three days. When that phase is complete, only the four with the fewest total faults move forward to the "final four", where all previous faults are dropped so that everyone starts with a clean slate. This "final four" takes place on the fourth and final day of competition.

On the final day the competition arena is set up differently from on the first three days. It is divided by a fence about a third of the way down the length of the ring. In the smaller end is a schooling area that consists of just two jumps next to each other, one is a vertical, and the other is an oxer. The remaining two-thirds of the ring holds a somewhat shortened Grand Prix course. When the final competition begins, all four horse/rider combinations enter the ring and remain there for the duration of the competition.

Each rider jumps the course on his or her own horse. They can prepare only by schooling over the two jumps in the schooling area. They can jump the oxer twice and the vertical twice, but then they must enter the ring and jump the course. A whistle signals them when they have one minute left to enter the ring. The riders then switch horses until each of the four competitors has ridden everyone else's horse. So, on a horse that they most likely have never ridden, they get to jump a maximum of four schooling fences, and then negotiate a Grand Prix course. This is all being done in front of the entire horse world. The WEG is an incredibly exciting event, but very taxing on the riders and especially the horses. A horse that makes it through the finals will have jumped nine world-class courses in four days, an extraordinary effort to ask of a horse.

In 2002, Peter and Fein Cera qualified to represent the United States at the WEG in Jerez, Spain. Due to the extreme summer heat in that part of Spain, it was scheduled for late September. Fran and I were still managing Ox Ridge Hunt Club at the time. We tried to put a plan together to go and support Peter because we knew what an honor this was for him. We also wanted to show support for Ray Texel in his first World Championship. Ray had worked for us at ORHC and was now based in California. We had become good friends during our time together. Unfortunately, the WEG schedule conflicted with the Maclay regional for our area. We couldn't abandon our riders who were fortunate enough to qualify that year, so Fran and I decided to split up. Fran would stay and train our riders at the regional, and I would go to Spain. Annie, who was already living in Belgium hoped to go as well, so I decided to make it a father, daughter vacation. Julia was able to clear her schedule, and the two of us headed to Spain to meet Annie and cheer Peter on to victory.

The first obstacle that we encountered is that Jerez is a fairly rural area without very many hotel rooms, so we had to stay 40 minutes away in Seville and rent a car. I was a bit irritated at having to stay that distance until we got to Seville and saw how beautiful and full of life the city was. Our hotel was an older Spanish-style complex with a center courtyard. Everywhere you walked in the city were cobblestone streets and outdoor cafes, and the food was fantastic. Each restaurant seemed better than the one before. It turned out to be an ideal place to stay, and we were certainly not alone, it seemed as if most of the American contingent was also there. While we were dealing with what we thought was going to be a problem but wasn't, Peter was facing a real problem.

Before every F.E.I.-sanctioned event, the horses are all jogged for soundness in front of the F.E.I. steward and the official veterinarian. A horse that does not pass can be presented again, but all must jog sound within a reasonable time. With some horses the official jog is always a question. Like any athlete, some have nagging injuries that have to be nursed along during the show season, and as they grow older, some horses have issues that need constant attention. The F.E.I. has a no medication policy, which makes it even more difficult for some horses on the day of the jog. Any horse that does not pass cannot compete. In addition, a horse can be disqualified at any time during the competition if they are judged to be unsound.

Thursday's official jog went as usual with Fein Cera jogging sound. The next morning, however, things took a bad turn. When Peter brought Cera out for the scheduled schooling session, she was sore, something which was very unusual for Cera. Peter had to scratch from the warm-up. Fortunately, with cold-water hosing and hand walking, by the afternoon, she was sound again. The warm-up went all day due to the large number of riders, so Peter was able to ride near the end, and Cera was sound and jumped beautifully. We were not yet at Jerez when it happened, but I can imagine what Peter was going through.

When you are part of a team for an event like the World Championship or the Olympics, you have to think in terms of "team first". Although this was Peter's first World Championships and he would do anything to take part, he dreaded letting the team down. Once Fein Cera went in the opening round, if she went lame and couldn't continue, the team would not be able to substitute its alternate rider. Peter wanted to make sure the team thought that he and Fein Cera were their best combination. Peter called the other team members together and asked them to vote by secret ballot if they wanted he and Fein Cera to represent the team. This was a very unusual thing to do, but Peter wanted to be sure. They voted unanimously to keep Peter and Fein Cera on the team. Long after the games were over, Peter would be honored for his unselfishness by being awarded the Whitney Stone Sportsmanship Cup (as an interesting side bar, Whitney Stone, the long-time USET supporter, had introduced Peter's parents many years before).

The girls and I were not able to get to Jerez until the last day of qualifying. We called Peter on his cell phone, and met up with him outside the stadium. Peter felt badly that he could not get passes for us. The organizers were being very tight with credentials and security, and since his parents were also there, Peter couldn't manage to get enough for all of us to sit together. Annie, Julia and I had already purchased seats online, so it was not a major problem. It would have been fun to all sit together, though. We made a plan to meet Peter inside, so that we could walk the course.

Although the seating had not turned out as perfectly as we had hoped, the important part of the week was going great. Peter and Cera were nearly perfect in the first four rounds of qualifying. They were leading the entire field with only 1.55 penalty points. That represented only time faults; they had not knocked down a single jump. They had been so good that in the final qualifying round they could knock down two rails for a total of 8 additional penalty points and still make the final four. They were the talk of the Championships.

We went inside the stadium early so we could look around. It was a beautiful venue, built especially for the WEG in an area of Andalusia famous for olives and especially for fine sherry. It was an open stadium with two levels of seating that held between twenty and thirty thousand people. It was early, so the stands were only about half full, but before the first horse went, they would be packed. The Europeans' love for all horse sport, but especially show jumping, is legendary. Our seats were in the balcony, but in the first row, so they were actually quite good. We put our jackets on the seats so people could see they were occupied, and then headed down stairs to walk the course. We walked separately from Peter because we didn't want to say or do anything might make him nervous. He was walking with the great Conrad Homfeld, who in recent years has helped Peter at the major international competitions. Conrad was the Team Gold and Individual Silver Medalist at the 1984 Los Angeles Olympics. He has tremendous insight and is always calm, or at least appears to be, which is perfect for Peter.

The gigantic jumps had been custom-made for WEG and were constructed and painted to represent something about the host country. Each jump was beautifully decorated with flowers and shrubs. The footing seemed really firm, almost hard under my feet. It was the first time I had seen the white sand that has become the favored footing in Europe.

I walked the course with one question in my mind: where could Peter get into trouble serious enough to have more than eight faults? As long as he could stay out of that kind of jam, he stood an excellent chance of making the final four.

As I walked around one end of the ring, there it was, right in front of me - an imposing triple combination. Cera was sometimes nervous in combinations, and this one was a monster. Not only did the distances walk long and the oxers measure wide, the standards had been built as three sections of wall, descending in height from over six feet down to approximately five feet. Each section was about five feet wide. From one end to the other, each element of the triple was over forty feet in width. Viewed from the front, the entire obstacle just looked like a huge indistinguishable mass. It would take a brave and trusting horse to carry its rider into this maze. Peter would encounter it about halfway through the course. If he and Cera cleared that point with no faults, I reasoned, they would be in great shape to make the final four. Once in the final four, everyone would start over with no faults, a clean slate. We completed walking the course, and returned to our seats. I sat between Annie and Jules.

Many of the competitors had been eliminated by the third day. Only the top twenty- five riders were invited to jump in the final qualifying round. They returned in reverse order, meaning that Peter and Cera would be the final pair to compete. Many of the early riders had serious problems with the course. Then, as the class drew closer to the end and the riders carrying fewer faults jumped, the course didn't seem quite so formidable. Dermott Lennon from Ireland had an excellent trip. Helena Lundback of Sweden, certainly the surprise of the event also was strong, disproving the "experts" who were sure she would wilt under the pressure. France's Eric Navet, for many years among the best in the world, was clear.

After what seemed like an eternity, the gates opened and Peter and Fein Cera entered the arena. Annie, Julia and I simultaneously leaned forward and clasped hands. Peter and Cera looked fantastic, but started a little slowly, I thought. Each jump was a huge effort. The two girls and I rose and sank back down as Fein Cera cleared each fence, as if trying to help.

By the third jump, they seemed to hit another gear, and everything appeared effortless. Perhaps Peter had forgotten his nerves and just started to ride. The triple combination that I was concerned about was on the side of the arena headed right toward us, and it was next. I squeezed the girls' hands a little tighter for luck. As the pair approached the first element, you could see Cera was questioning what to do. Great horses are incredible. They will study a jump on approach, with one thing on their mind, "how can I get over this thing that's in my way - how can I jump it clean". They really try to figure it out. It was obvious, though, that Cera was a little confused by this one. She crawled up and over the first element with Peter urging her forward with everything he had. They made a huge effort and barely skimmed the second element. It all seemed to be happening in slow motion. One final thrust, the rail bounced in the cups of the final element but stayed up. They were through it with no faults. "That-a boy, Pete" I said in a loud whisper. Six more jumps and they would be home. At last they headed toward the final obstacle with a clean round. They barely rolled the last rail and had it down, but it didn't matter, they were in. He did it! The three of us stood up and began cheering.

The final four would be: Eric Navet, Helena Lundback, Dermott Lennon and Peter. I gave the girls a hug, and we headed down the stairs to find Peter.

A celebratory dinner was planned at the host hotel that evening. Seddon and John Wylde made a fairly early reservation for our group. We wanted to all be together for this wonderful moment, but there was a long way to go before any real celebration. The final four would begin in a few hours, and since there are only three medals, someone was going home without one.

Annie, Jules and I arrived at the front door of the elegant host hotel and had our identification checked against the guest list. Only riders, owners and guests were allowed entrance to the hotel during the week of WEG. It was incredible to see the greatest riders from all over the world just milling around talking and joking with each other in the lobby of this grand old hotel. They all seemed so relaxed. I suppose for all but four, they could relax. They had given it everything they had, but all that was left to do now was to enjoy watching the finals.

We were all seated at a long banquet style table. Our group included Peter and his family, the three Dotolis, and Conrad Homfeld, who was training Peter at the WEG. We were enjoying a wonderful dinner when something really amazing happened, something beyond explanation. Peter was finishing his meal, when he raised his eyes and looked up at me. "Joe", he asked, "Today, when I jumped the last element of the triple combination, did you say 'that-a boy, Pete'?" I was speechless. We were sitting in the upper deck of a thirty thousand seat stadium, that was filled to capacity, and he heard me say, in a loud whisper, "that-a boy, Pete". "You heard that?" I asked. "Like you were the only one there" was Peter's reply. I paused a few seconds, too stunned to speak. Then I said, "So, what did you think?" Peter leaned back in his chair, flashed a big smile and said "I thought, 'shut the hell up, I've got half a course left to jump'." Then he roared laughing. I went back to the hotel that night with a new appreciation of that special connection between teacher and student. There is a unique bond that develops from all those years of being "tuned in" to each other during countless competitions.

Peter and "Fein Cera" at the 2002 World Equestrian Games, Jerez, Spain. Photo courtesy of Diana DeRosa Photography

The next day at the games, it became clear to me that Peter was put at a disadvantage by his own training style and his love of horses. His natural ability is as good as anyone, but what sets him apart at this world-class level is how he trains his horses and his connection to them. He can jump on any horse and ride it well, but if he gets a chance to work with that horse on a day-to-day basis, if he can put a horse into his program, then it becomes special. I suppose this is why he seems to always get the horses that others can't get along with; the tense ones, the stoppers, or the runaways. Even Cera had a reputation of being somewhat difficult, but look at her now. I should have realized that the WEG format would not be easy for him, having to get on strange horses with little preparation and then compete.

The competition started much the way it had ended the day before. All four riders were clean on their own horses. Peter and Cera were perfect, so smooth they could have been competing in the Maclay finals. However, switching horses with the other riders became a bit more difficult. Peter had rails on both Eric Navet's horse and Helena Lundback's horse. He rode beautifully, and ended up in third place, taking home the bronze medal, the first American to medal at the WEG since 1986.

During the day I had noticed that Peter schooled the other riders' horses far less than the rest of the competitors, he only jumped one or two jumps. Also, while the other riders had each horse tacked up by their groom, Peter handled and tacked each horse himself even though his groom was right there. When I asked him about it later, he replied, "They all worked so hard, I didn't want to overdo it," adding "I only had a few minutes to get to know each one, so I thought it would be better if I handled them myself". On the world's biggest stage, at the most important moment of his professional career, Peter thought of the horses first and his own success second. I smiled and shook my head a little. I was not surprised.

The biggest accolades of the week were saved for Fein Cera. She was named "Best Horse at the Finals." At the highest level of equestrian sport, her star had shown the brightest. Competing over nine world class courses, she knocked down a total of <u>one</u> rail, the meaningless one at the last jump on the last day of qualifying. It was a performance for the ages. Peter was more proud of her award than he was of his own.

Peter and "Fein Cera" victory lap at the 2002 World Equestrian
Games, Jerez Spain. Photo courtesy of Charles Mann Photography.

The 2002
Equestrian of the Year

As 2002 was coming to an end, I received a phone call from Peter, who wanted to know if I was going to the USEF convention. He was not able to leave Europe because of a very important show that week. In Europe, the "A" list riders are invited to the big shows. Being invited means you get a lot of monetary incentives. It also means, you had better be there if you want to be invited again.

At that time, I was on the Board of Directors of the USEF, so I was planning on making the trip to Lexington Kentucky. "Will you be at the Pegasus Dinner"? Peter asked. The Pegasus dinner is a grand affair where all the year-end awards are presented. I said that I was going, even though before he called I was considering giving it a pass. "Could you do something for me there", he asked. "Of course, what is it"? "Could you pick up an award for me"? "They're giving me equestrian of the year".

"That's great Pete, congratulations", I said.

Peter continued, "Could you read something for me"?

"You're setting me up, aren't you" I said, kidding him.

"No, but I'll send you a shorter acceptance if you don't want to read the longer one. I'll fax it to you when you get to the hotel". Peter was not kidding, and I wondered what was up.

It was a great year for Peter. After winning the bronze medal at WEG, he was named Equestrian of the Year by *The Chronicle of the Horse*, and now the same honor by the United States Equestrian Federation, the governing body of equestrian sport in the U.S. I was very proud of him. He epitomizes what it means to be a horseman.

The only thing left at the convention after the Pegasus dinner is the Board of Directors meeting the next morning. At that meeting all the rule changes that were talked about endlessly during the convention are voted on by the board. Most of them are not very contentious, but every year there are a few that stir things up. One of the more controversial changes this year was a proposed rule which would allow junior riders to compete without braiding their horses.

To people outside the horse world this would not seem like a big deal, but the horse world is very deep in tradition and we adhere to our past to an almost absurd degree. And although not braiding would seem like a small thing, it is really not. It is quite expensive, and must be done, and undone every day if it is to look right. Professional braiders work all night in the stable area, and are very well compensated for their efforts.

In the past, riders, especially junior riders, would braid their own horses. Today, however, most junior riders would not know how to begin braiding, many of them even consider it below them. Frustrated with the cost and lack of interest from the riders, some trainers had gotten together and proposed this rule change. I must admit to being intrigued by the idea, and was considering voting for it although it went against my instincts as a horseman, mostly because the cost of braiding had gotten so ridiculous.

It was getting late on the night of the Pegasus dinner and I still had not received a fax from Peter. I figured if it didn't come I could just fake it. After all, how many ways were there to say "thank you for this very prestigious award"? If it failed to arrive, I would make something up on the fly.

When dinner was over, we all sat attentively while the awards were given out. Equestrian of the Year is among the most prestigious, so it is one of the last presented. Finally, the master of ceremonies announced, "Equestrian of the Year goes to Mr. Peter Wylde. Accepting the award for Peter, who was unable to attend, is his long-time trainer and friend Mr. Joe Dotoli".

As I walked from the table along the side of the room, I passed a door that led to the lobby. A hotel employee handed me some papers and said, "This came for you a little while ago". I glanced down to see a fax cover sheet from Peter. "That's cutting it a little close" I thought.

I got to the microphone without having a chance to get ready, so I told the audience that I was going to read a prepared statement from Peter. I could see there were two, as he had promised, so I started reading the longer one. I was not very far into it, when I began to get choked up. I was afraid I would not be able to finish it, but I did.

I have kept that fax since that night because it means a great deal to both Fran and me. This was what Peter had to say when he was named "Equestrian of the Year".

> First, I'd like to say that this is a tremendous honor. I have always respected the recipients of this award, and regarded this as a lifetime achievement of great significance. 2002 was an unbelievable year for me. It was filled with incredible stress and pressure, but also an equal amount of reward. The results of 2002 came to me in large part because of a special horse named Fein Cera. She is the most outstanding animal I have ever worked with. She is the kind of horse that riders and trainers dream about, making our work seem easy. For this I feel very fortunate.

> There is something else which makes me feel very fortunate, which I'd like to take this opportunity to share. I was recently reading an issue of The *Chronicle of the Horse* where I was confused to read a proposed rule change, asking for junior hunters to be allowed not to be braided. This was something that in a way concerned me, but then actually made me happy. I competed at 20 international competitions this year including the World Championships. I took three to four horses to every competition. I braided them all myself, for every class. The proposed rule change confused me because I didn't understand why juniors couldn't braid their own horses if the argument is that braiding is too expensive. And then, upon reflection, I was reminded of how lucky I was to have grown up in Fran and Joe's stable. As juniors, we all took care of our own horses; braided, bandaged, clipped, lunged, and fed them. They were our responsibility. We were allowed, encouraged or better yet expected to learn to do all this ourselves. Of course we made mistakes, and maybe our braids didn't look perfect, but we became good horse people. We spent time with our horses and learned about them. This made us better riders.

If I am to receive an award for my horsemanship, I owe it in large part to my upbringing. I feel very fortunate to have been expected to braid my horses when I was younger and hope that I will be able to do so for the rest of my career as a horseman. For this award, I am honored and give my sincerest thanks.

There was a tremendous round of applause. I was so angry at myself for considering voting in favor of this rule. Peter had reminded me what was right, the same way he did that early morning at Harrisburg many years ago when he wouldn't let Tracy take over bathing The Wolf just because it was late and he needed to get some sleep before the Medal Finals the next day. He learned his lessons well, and they are not negotiable. The next morning, although it had seemed certain to pass, the "no braiding" rule was defeated 50 – 0 by the Board of Directors of The United States Equestrian Federation.

The 2004 Olympic Games
Athens, Greece

Most talented young riders have a number of goals they want to achieve during their careers, but one always one stands above all the others; going to the Olympics. Peter was no different. Ever since he was a boy, he dreamed about representing the United States in the Olympic Games. Now, in 2004, with a bronze medal from the World Games on his resume' and the "horse of a lifetime" in his stable, he finally had his chance. His place on the team was certainly not a given, he would have to come to the States for the selection trials, but barring any unforeseen disasters, he had to be considered a front-runner.

The first problem was getting Fein Cera to the United States for the Trials. She is a good shipper in a horse van, but she hates to fly. With the Atlantic Ocean between her and the trials, there weren't many options. Peter, always taking responsibility for the well being of his horses, flew in the belly of the plane with her. Cera arrived a little down on her weight but otherwise unscathed.

Peter and Cera performed as advertised and made the team for Athens along with; McLain Ward and the chestnut mare Sapphire, Chris Kappler on the magnificent bay stallion Royal Kaliber and Beezie Madden with the bay gelding Authentic. Frank Chapot would again serve as Chef d'Equipe. The U.S. couldn't have asked for more; four great riders, all with resumes that included a great deal of international success, and four proven horses of world class ability. Hopes were high as the games approached.

Fran and I began making plans to go to the Olympic Games in Athens. I strongly recommend that anyone who is given the opportunity to go to the Olympics as a spectator take full advantage of it. I have been lucky enough to attend five; Munich '72, Montreal '76, Los Angeles '84, Atlanta '96, and Athens '04. Each was an amazing adventure. I have gone mainly to see the equestrian games, but have always managed to fit in a number of other events and they are all worth seeing. There is no other sporting event like it.

We did some of the planning on our own, and used a travel agent for the remainder. We got our plane tickets, and were a little shocked by the high price tag, but we figured the airlines would take advantage of a captive audience. We then bought tickets to the events themselves, and again, sticker shock, (it had been a while since we went to an Olympics). Finally, we shopped for accommodations. That appeared to be the "deal breaker". We checked a number of possibilities, and for two hotel rooms (our daughter Annie was meeting us there); the price was 500-700 Euros per night per room. With a little multiplication and the exchange rate at the time the rooms came to about $15,000 for the two weeks. I looked at Fran. "We can't do this" I said. "There is no way we can justify this". Fran nodded agreement, her disappointment was obvious.

When we called Seddon Wylde to tell her we weren't coming, she had an idea. "Call MacRae", she encouraged, "he has rented a boat". Peter's brother, MacRae, and his wife Ellen are in the sailing industry on the West Coast. Through their connections, we were given a contact in Greece who owned a charter company. Sometimes things just work out. Instead of living in a cramped, non-air conditioned hotel room for two weeks, we would be living on a 54-foot sailboat with two state-rooms, private baths, a living area and a galley. It was also a small fraction of the cost of a hotel. We were going to Greece after all.

We headed to Athens, determined to take in as much as the ancient city as we could possibly manage in two short weeks. As soon as we landed we took a cab directly to Athens harbor where our "hotel" was docked. The sight was incredible. I think every boat owner in the Mediterranean had decided to rent their boats for the Games - I called it the "boat ghetto". The boats were all lashed together side by side with planks leading from one to another. We were very fortunate; our boat was a permanent resident of the marina and was "tied up" with its stern to the dock. We had to "walk the plank" to our boat too, but it was just one plank, from the dock to the boat. Some people had to criss-cross over several planks to get to their designated boat. It made for a really fun atmosphere, however, with everyone helping each other.

The political atmosphere during the summer of 2004 was not a particularly good one for Americans traveling abroad. We were warned about possible terror groups planning attacks on Americans at the Games. The giant security blimp floating above the harbor was a constant reminder of the potential for danger. The rumor was that it was equipped with a billion dollars worth of high tech monitoring equipment, that if you were reading the morning paper, the security people could read it just as easily. "Big brother at its best", I thought. There were supposedly three blimps. This one spent a great deal of time over the harbor, probably because many of the athletes were being housed in great cruise ships anchored there. Navy Seals patrolled the area to protect against attacks from the water.

The marina had people from every imaginable country. It was a very fun and friendly place. All the boats proudly flew the flag of their homeland, with the exception of the American flag. We were advised before we got there that for safety reasons flying the US flag would not be a good idea. We were warned that it might make our boat a target for terrorists. In the beginning we did as we were told, and apparently so did all the other Americans. There was no sign of the stars and stripes anywhere, but then an interesting thing happened, one by one American flags started popping up. Each day when we awoke there would be one here, another there. I am proud to say our boat was one of the very first to raise the colors. By the end of the first week, it seemed like half the boats were occupied by Americans. For all the talk about how much animosity there was toward the US at that time, there certainly was no sign of it in Athens. I guess that is what the Olympics are supposed to be all about.

Another thing that became obvious was that all the stories in the media about Athens and the Greek government not being prepared were totally incorrect. If they were still in the middle of construction weeks before the start of the Games, it certainly didn't look it on day one. All the construction not only appeared complete, but beautifully done. Markopoulo Equestrian Center, built especially for the games, was an hour's ride from the city, but it was worth the drive and then some. It was a fabulous outdoor stadium. The jumps told the story of Greece, both ancient and modern. It was thrilling to be in the country where the Olympics began. The only thing people were questioning was the decision of the organizers to have grass instead of all-weather footing. As a concession to the Greek climate, the equestrian events, (actually most of the outdoor events) were held either early in the morning or in the evening.

The first day of jumping was a qualifier for the individual medals, but not for the teams. We were seated with all of Peter's family, in hats that his mom gave us that had "Peter Wylde" and "Fein Cera" embroidered on them. We all proudly wore them. That morning as we watched Peter and Conrad walk the course, Fran and I both thought Peter looked very nervous. Later that day we found out that as he walked the combination in front of us, he couldn't look up for fear he would "lose it". As Peter and Conrad walked past a jump fairly close to us, I flashed Peter the "thumbs up" sign, and mouthed, "You're going to be great". He smiled, and kept walking.

Peter and Conrad Homfeld walking the course at the 2004 Olympic Games, Athens, Greece. Photo courtesy of the author.

**Peter at 2004 Olympic Games, Athens, Greece. Photo
courtesy of Diana DeRosa Photography.**

After what seemed like a hundred rounds, Peter and Fein Cera entered the Olympic stadium. It was an awesome feeling to realize that we were sitting at the Olympics watching Peter ride for the United States. I had goose-bumps, we all did. The two of them cruised around the course as if they were jumping a hunter course back home. The last jump, situated to our left at the opposite end of the arena, was a huge oxer. As soon as Fein Cera cleared it, Peter leaned forward and galloped through the finish line to trip the electronic timers. No faults - they were clean. Then he turned and galloped across the stadium. As he approached where we were sitting, he broke into a huge smile and flashed us the "thumbs up" sign. (That wonderful moment was frozen in time by photographer Charles Mann and graces the cover of this book). What a perfect start to Peter and Cera's Olympic debut.

The equestrian events are not scheduled everyday, and the next day was an off day. We headed out to see some of the other events and do some sightseeing. We saw the double overtime win for the American women in the soccer finals against Brazil, where Mia Hamm showed everyone why she is the greatest to ever play the game. Although we couldn't get tickets to the swimming venue, we did get into a number of other sports.

By far the most emotional moment for me, outside Markopoulo Arena, came at an evening performance in the main Olympic Stadium. The arena was packed, mostly with Greeks, with over 100,000 people. A Greek woman named Fani Halkia was one of the favorites in the women's 400-meter hurdles. As the runners were pulling off their sweat suits to prepare for the start, the crowd began to chant, "Hellas, Hellas, Hellas" over and over ("Hellas" means "Greece"). When the athletes took their mark it grew even louder. The starter's gun echoed through the stadium, and the chanting was at a fever pitch. Everyone was chanting "Hellas", Greeks and non-Greeks including Fran and me. The 400-meter hurdles is not a long race, a little over 50 seconds. When Feni Halkia crossed the finish line and won Greece's first gold medal the scene was something you will only see at the Olympic Games. I can not imagine what that woman must have been feeling.

The next day of jumping was the team competition. All four Americans would ride. In team jumping the round with the highest faults gets dropped from the total at the end. It is referred to as the "drop score". A country that has only three riders can still compete, but all three scores count. Because of this "drop score", a team total can change dramatically when the last horse goes. The scores in the team competition also count toward the individual total. The opening-day round plus the two rounds of the team competition are added together, and only the best 45 move on to the individual finals. Also, no country is allowed more than three riders in the individual final. This was a concern for the Americans because all four were definitely capable of being among the top forty five riders. Peter had a great start with a clean round the first day.

One of the duties of the Chef d'Equipe is to determine the order of go for the team. The most experienced rider generally goes last, much like a clean-up hitter in baseball, and the second most experienced one goes first to get the team off to a good start. Frank Chapot decided that Beezie Madden would go last and Peter would lead off.

Left to right: Fran, Joe and Annie Dotoli at the Athens Olympics. Photo courtesy of the author.

When the rotation finally came to the first American pair, Peter and Fein Cera, our group rose and cheered wildly. They galloped across the arena, then came down to a walk. We settled back into our seats. The stadium grew silent, the 45-second horn sounded, Peter took one last look around to review the course, and then they were off. The beginning went well but then they ran into problems. Cera had a foot in the water for four faults (a foot in the water is scored the same as a rail down), which seemed to unsettle her. They had one rail down, then a second, Peter managed to hold it together, but the twelve faults that they accumulated was definitely not the start the team was hoping for. When Peter came back to see us he was very upset, almost inconsolable. He was not so much upset that he had a poor round, but because he felt he let the team down. Their placing going into the final round came down to the last rotation, and Beezie showed very emphatically why she was the final rider. Her clear round meant that Peter's twelve faults could be the drop score. The Americans were still right in the middle of the fight.

The second round did not go any better for Peter and Fein Cera. Again they had a twelve fault score, and again Peter was very upset at the idea that he was letting his team down. This time the score had an even more serious consequence because it meant that Peter would probably not qualify for the individual competition. Not because his scores would not have qualified, but because of the rule allowing only three from any one team. Fortunately, Beezie was again unbelievable. She jumped clean and kept the Americans in the race. Peter was happy for the team, but understandably disappointed in his own performance.

After a brief wait, the results were posted; the Germans were way ahead in first place, the Americans were tied with Sweden for the silver and bronze medals. There would be a jump off to decide between the two. A chance for redemption; Peter would get one more round to try to help his team. I was so happy. I didn't want him to end his Olympic experience feeling like he had not contributed.

Down in the schooling area the three young men on the team - McLain, Chris and Peter - made a pact to get the job done. After all Beezie had already accomplished, she should not have to repeat her performance a third time. With a renewed sense of determination, Peter mounted up for what would be his last ride of the 2004 Olympics. He had two jobs. First, he was to go clean and, not to worry about going fast, but to start the team off with a solid round. His second assignment was to see whether a very tricky speed turn was possible. There was an arrangement of artificial boulders and plants in a line keeping riders from making the turn to the last jump, but they were not flagged, so legally they could be jumped. Nobody walked the turn because they didn't want to give away their plan. As Peter cantered around them, he was to see if it was possible.

Peter and Fein Cera galloped into the arena and then came down to a walk. You could hear a pin drop. The horn sounded, and they were off. They were really moving, but in control and smoothly. They galloped around the turn to the last oxer with no faults. They sailed over the last jump effortlessly. They were through the timers clean, <u>and</u> fast. When I looked up at the clock I couldn't believe their time - 45.66 seconds. That would be tough to beat, what a great start for the team. I could only imagine the weight that must have been lifted off Peter. Because he had reported back to the team that the tough turn could be made, both McLain and Chris made the difficult turn. Both jumped clean and both were incredibly fast. The Swedish team was so far back that their final pair did not even ride because the time difference was insurmountable. The Americans won the silver medal (soon to be replaced by gold).

Seeing Peter on the podium receiving his silver medal was such a great feeling. He and his other teammates were smiling and waving. They wore the ancient Greek wreaths that all medal-winners were adorned with for the ceremonies. You could see how happy and proud all four of them were. My eyes were filled with tears of joy, and I know I wasn't alone.

In the weeks and months that followed Athens, two things happened that changed how those Olympics will be remembered by people in the horse world. Chris Kappler went on to win an individual bronze medal, but at a terrible cost. In a jump-off for the silver medal, Chris's great stallion, Royal Kaliber, took a bad step and came up very lame. Chris retired and was awarded the bronze medal. The on-site care for Royal Kaliber was excellent- veterinarians and a horse ambulance were there instantly. Initially it didn't seem that his injuries were career-or life-threatening, but they were. After a gallant fight, Royal Kaliber died, not from his injuries at Athens, but from complications from colic surgery. He was a great horse.

The second thing that happened was that the United States was eventually awarded team gold medals. One member of the German team's horse was disqualified for failing a drug test. The German total, using their "drop score" was still good enough to hold on to the bronze, but the Americans were elevated to gold.

**The Wylde Family at the Athens Olympics. Left to right:
Ellen (sister-in-law), Seddon (mom), Fiona (neice), Peter and
MacRae (brother). Photo courtesy of the author.**

Epilogue

After Peter won the Maclay, I thought we were going to win every year. I thought we had it all figured out. It took a long time to realize how difficult it is to get all those variables to line up. We came close a few more times: Mia Wood was Reserve Champion at the Medal Finals in 1984, and our daughter Annie was third in the Maclay in 1991. We had numerous other ribbons, and five regional New England Medal Champions, but Peter's win remains our only national equitation championship. Yet, when I think of all the terrific trainers we know who have never won a finals, and many who have never even had a ribbon, I realize how fortunate we have been.

I believe the true success Fran and I have had in the sport lies in the number of young riders that came through our barn and are still involved with horses on some level. We instilled in our riders a love of horses and a connection to them. We were able to keep the stress of competition from detracting from the experience of riding by focusing on the horses and not simply on winning a ribbon. I like to win as much as anyone, but if you don't enjoy your horses along the way, you miss out on the best part. I'm also proud that most of our former riders credit the discipline they got from horses and riding as being a big part of their accomplishments in life.

When the Maclay Finals were at the Garden, the trucks carrying the equitation horses were not allowed to park on the street until after midnight. The horses had to stand on the trucks until schooling started early in the morning. Sometimes you could sneak in a little early, but around 11:30 P.M. the horse vans started lining up on 33rd Street, an unusual sight, to say the least. Our system was for Fran to get to bed early, while I waited up for the horses and then got to "sleep in", at least until 5:00 A.M. Through the years it became a tradition for our former students to come back from college or wherever they might be and wait with me for the horses to arrive. We always met in the same place; Charlie O's restaurant and bar located under the Garden on 33rd Street. We told stories of the "old" days and had a lot of laughs. Connecting with those kids was always a treat for me, and a good reminder of the value of our life's work.

The year after Peter won the Maclay , I entered Charlie O's about 9:30 P.M. and saw two of our former students, Beth McCombs (Westvold) and Nancy Norlie (Flynn), and joined them at their booth. Charlie O's had very comfortable horse-shoe shaped booths, with high padded leather backs. It was a great place to spend time waiting for the horses. When I glanced across the room, I saw Peter deep in conversation with a young woman who had won the Maclay a few years earlier. I had not seen her since. Peter and she were friends, so the scene was not very unusual except that she was crying. They talked for quite a long time.

When Peter finally made his way over to our booth, he sat next to me. "What was that all about", I asked him.

"She wanted to know if I still loved it, if I still loved to ride," Peter replied. When I said yes, she began to cry. She said that she really envied me, that by the time she won, she couldn't wait for it to be over. I guess the pressure just got to her".

So many times you hear that an athlete ends up hating the sport they love so much because of the pressure to win at the highest level. In the equitation division, that feeling is intensified by it all coming to an end at 17 years old. Young riders usually start bragging about how many years of equitation are left in their junior careers; "I have seven years left, I have six years left" and so on. At some point the mind-set changes, and so does the terminology: "I *only* have three years left, I *only* have two years left". It is a major psychological difference. To make the situation worse, parents often start repeating the mantra.

If winning one of the finals is the only thing that can bring happiness and satisfaction, then only three riders a year will be productive. But, if you enjoy your horse and get satisfaction from what you can teach him and what you can accomplish together, and thrive on the competition that comes with it, then you can have a lifetime of satisfaction. Equitation is *not* the end product. It is the means to an end, the American system of teaching young people to become good riders and horsemen. If a young rider wins one of the finals but doesn't understand his or her horse and what went into that success, then I believe they have missed the whole point.

Even though the era of professional grooms at most barns has made it more difficult to become a good horseman, those that seek it out and work toward that goal will be well rewarded. Not so long ago, juniors took care of their own horses at home and away at shows. At some point it became more cost-effective to have professional grooms and braiders. Things were done much faster, and there was less trainer supervision required. Somewhere along the way, however, a good deal of the connection between horse and rider got lost. When Peter braids his own horse for the Olympics or the World Games, it's not because he can't afford to pay a braider. He could have any braider he wants. He does the braiding himself because it is his time to connect, to focus, and to reflect. When Major Mike worked with us at camp, we were all required as part of our routine to hand-graze our horses at 3:00 P.M. every day. We had plenty of paddocks, but this was our time to connect with our horses. Mike called it taking your horse for "sal-a-a-a-d". He would drag the word out. Those are precious memories for me.

Horses, particularly equitation horses, are an incredibly kind and forgiving group. I hope we always remember that and guard against taking advantage of their generosity. A young person who is learning to ride must execute exercises over and over, day after day. Even though the good old equitation horses could do most of those exercises with their eyes closed, they continue to repeat them without complaint.

Many years ago, in 1983, I wrote a poem for the retirement of CeCe Zack's great equitation horse, Old Salt, whose barn name was Mort. The poem summarizes my feelings about these wonderful and giving creatures. I hope you enjoy it.

The Equitation Horse

Seldom an elegant mover,
rarely jumps in great form,
often a workman-like beauty,
but never a threat to conform.
He wears the rewards of caring,
he's puffed and pulled and worn.
Though admired by all those who know him,
few would know his show name,
but that barn name means plenty
to those who know the best; Surf, or Mort, or Rags.

He's the one we need most,
and the hardest to find,
and the good ones we fight hard to keep.
With all his short comings,
and all that he lacks,
what is it that makes this one special?
He's got stride, must have – and plenty.
Size, almost always has that,
but what makes him great is neither of these,
and hard to define as a trait.
Some call it heart, some attitude,
and some will just say he tries.
He'll absorb all the pain,
spend days in the van,
suffer mistakes and forgive.
He'll teach them to ride,
get them qualified,
and take them around at New York.
Then when they've matured,
the odds they'll ignore,
and head to the finals for fame.
Then when that one is done,
and the tears have all run,
he'll go on to the next one in line.
She's just off a pony, and little bit scared,
this one needs plenty of help.
One more year 'n those old feet will hurt even more,
time has taken it's toll.
He's jumped more jumps than any horse should,
in mud and on pavement hard ground.
And though no one has asked if he'd like to retire,
there really isn't a need.
When the braiding begins before it gets light,
and the roar of the van breaks the quiet of night.
When the gate at The Garden swings open wide,
and a young heart pounds with fear it can't hide.
To answer the question - retire or show him,
just look in those wise and knowing old eyes,
and love him for all that we owe him.

Glossary

Amateur-Owner hunter – A division at the horse shows reserved for amateurs, over 18 years old who own their own horses. The division is closed to professionals.

Bedding - The material that is put into a stall for a horse to sleep on. It can be wood shavings or straw, depending on the part of the country, but many other materials have been tried as well; shredded newspaper, peanut shells, vermiculite, peat moss, and many processed varieties.

Bit – The metal part of the bridle that goes in the horse's mouth.

Bran – Wheat or oat husks used to regulate the digestive tract. It has flakey, almost powdery consistency.

Bridle – The piece of equipment that goes on the horse's head. The bit and reins are attached to it.

Canter – The three-beat gait of a horse.

Chef d'Equipe – The person in charge of an international team. Most riders have their own coach, but the Chef d'Equipe organizes everything and is in charge of picking the jumping order for the team.

Chestnut – A reddish-brown colored horse or pony with similar mane and tail.

Chip – When a rider misjudges where to take off, and takes an short stutter-step stride in front of a fence. It is the same as a miss.

Clean – The score in a jumper class when a horse has no jumping faults (rails down or refusals) and no time faults for exceeding the time allowed.

Colic – Upset intestinal tract. There are several different types, all very serious conditions in horses because horses lack the musculature to vomit. Colic kills more horses than any other condition.

Counter-canter – Asking a horse to canter on the opposite or counter lead. For example; cantering on the left lead while tracking to the right.

Cross-rail – A jump constructed using two rails, each having one end in a cup and the other end on the ground to form an X.

Curry comb – A rubber utensil with an uneven surface that, when rubbed in a circular motion on a horse's coat, brings the dirt to the surface and stimulates the skin.

Drag the ring – To prepare this riding surface for competition by smoothing it.

Draw reins - Very long reins that go from the rider's hand, through the bit, and back to the girth. They are usually not used for showing, only for schooling. They give a rider a lot of leverage, and should only be used by experienced riders.

Dressage – A discipline where horses are trained to perform specific movements on the flat. It could be thought of as ballet for horses.

Drop noseband – A specialized noseband that is much lower on the horse's muzzle, just over the bit. It is used to keep a horse's mouth closed.

Element – Any individual jump in a combination of jumps.

Equitation Division – A competition in which the rider is judged on the style, and how he affects the horse, form as relates to function. The judging is subjective like figure skating or gymnastics.

European warm blood – Horses bred in Europe for sport. Just as we have been breeding excellent lines of race horses in this country for hundreds of years, the Europeans have been doing the same with sport horses.

F.E.I – Federation Equestrian Internationale – Governing body of International Equestrian sport.

Footing – The material in the ring that you ride on. It can be many different combinations of natural and artificial materials, including grass.

Forage – All grass feeds. When a horse walks around a pasture eating; he is foraging or grazing.

Forge – A fire pit where a blacksmith heats metal when making horse shoes. Today most of them are propane fired and travel with the blacksmith in the back of a pick up truck.

Founder – A condition affecting the lining of a horse's hoof; the lamina. It is extremely painful and can be career or even life threatening. It is also called Laminitis.

Girth – A heavy leather strap that holds the saddle in place.

Grand Prix jumping – The highest level of show jumping.

Green – An inexperienced horse or pony.

Grooming – Using brushes and a curry comb to clean and bring out the sheen in a horse's coat.

Hacking – To ride a horse on the flat (without jumping) with no training involved, just for exercise.

Hand – The unit used to measure horses. One hand is four inches. The measurement is taken from the ground next to the heel of one front foot, to the top of the withers.

Hay net – A bag made of rope that is filled with hay and hung so a horse can eat without having to reach down to the ground. They are often used in horse vans during transportation.

Hoof pick – A curved metal or plastic utensil that is used to remove the dirt and possibly stones from the under surface of the horse's foot.

Hunters – Horses that are judged on their style of jumping and the way they move. This discipline has evolved from fox hunting, although the similarities are mostly in the distant past. The judging is subjective, much like gymnastics, or figure skating.

Jump cup – An adjustable metal or plastic fixture that holds the rails or poles on a jump. It can be raised or lowered to change the height of the jump.

Jumpers – Horses that are judged on faults - knocking down a jump, or refusing to jump - and time. The judging is objective.

Junior rider – A rider under 18 years old.

Lame – Unsound, limping.

Large pony – A pony that measures over 13.2 hands, but not taller than 14.2 hands.

Lead – When a horse canters, it is the leg he starts each stride with. When cantering to the left he will lead with his left front leg, he is on the left lead.

Line – When there is a series of jumps in a row that are at least three strides apart. The rider must figure out how many strides his horse will take between those jumps. One or two strides is considered a combination rather than a line.

Maclay Finals – One of four national equitation championships for junior riders. It is sponsored by the A.S.P.C.A. (The American Society for the Prevention of Cruelty to Animals). The trophy is dedicated to the memory of Alfred B. Maclay.

Martingale – A strap of leather that goes from the noseband to the girth. It is used to keep a horse's head down.

Medal Finals – One of four national equitation finals for junior riders. It is held each October in Harrisburg, PA. It is sponsored by the United States Equestrian Federation, the governing body of equestrian sport (at the time of this story its name was the American Horse Shows Association).

Miss – see chip

Morgan horses – This is a breed of horse begun in Vermont by Justin Morgan. These horses are known for their versatility and strength. They are generally not very big, but can do a lot of jobs.

Mucking out – Cleaning a horse's stall.

Noseband – A strap of leather that goes around the horse's muzzle, a few inches above the bit.

Oxer – A jump that has height *and* width

Paddock – Another name of pasture, however, it is usually smaller.

Poultice – A compound applied to a horse's legs or feet that draws out heat and reduces swelling. There are a number of different kinds.

Reins –The leather straps that go from the bit in the horse's mouth to the rider's hand.

Saddle – The equipment that fits on the horse's back, where the rider sits. A good saddle can be very expensive, but is crucial to a horse's comfort.

Scopy – When a horse not only can jump a tall jump, but can also jump easily across very wide jumps.

Scratches – A condition where the area around and above a horse's heels gets cracked and sore. It can also easily get infected.

Snaffle bit – The least severe bit you can use. It consists of two pieces of metal jointed in the middle, and attached to rings on the sides where the bridle and reins are also attached.

Sound – Not lame.

Spooky – When a horse is unreasonably afraid of the things around him which he should be accustomed to.

Stall – The box where a horse lives in the barn. They are usually about 12' x 12'.

Stirrups – Where a rider puts his feet.

Stride – The distance a horse or pony covers in one cantering or galloping step.

Sweet feed – A mixed feed containing oats, corn, bran and molasses.

Tack – Any equipment that goes on the horse.

Tack-up – Put on your saddle and bridle.

Take a horse off your leg – To press your lower leg against your horse until he moves over.

Thoroughbred – The breed of horse used for racing. They are known for their exceptional speed and athleticism. In the past most show horses in America were thoroughbreds that had either completed their racing careers or simply were not fast enough to race. Today, the thoroughbred has been almost completely replaced in the show ring by European warm- bloods.

Three day event – An Olympic competition that was originally conceived to demonstrate the skills of the cavalry horse in battle. The name was later changed from the military event to the three day event. It involves a dressage test, a cross country jumping course and an enclosed stadium jumping course.

Time Allowed – After the course designer completes constructing his course he measures it and determines how long it *should* take to complete the course at a given speed. That is the time allowed, and if you exceed the time allowed you are penalized for each second over it.

Trot – The four-beat gait of a horse.

Twisted wire bit – The most severe type of snaffle bit. Sometimes called a wire W, it works on the corners of a horse's mouth.

Under saddle class – A class where there is no jumping. Horses walk, trot, and canter in both directions of the ring and are judged on how well they move.

Vertical – A jump that only has height, no width.

Withers – The bone at the base of the neck that is the highest point on a horse's back.

About the Author

Joe Dotoli lives in Vermont, on an island in Lake Champlain, with his wife Fran and their two dogs. They no longer operate a training stable, but stay very active in the horse industry judging horse shows, giving clinics, and being involved in horse show management. This is the author's first book.

The author. Photo courtesy of the author.